Harvard Business Review

on

ADVANCING YOUR CAREER

The Harvard Business Review
Paperback series

If you need the best practices and ideas for the business challenges you face—but don't have time to find them—*Harvard Business Review* **paperbacks** are for you. Each book is a collection of HBR's inspiring and useful perspectives on a given management topic, all in one place.

The titles include:

Harvard Business Review

on

ADVANCING YOUR CAREER

Harvard Business Review Press

Boston, Massachusetts

Copyright 2011 Harvard Business School Publishing Corporation

All rights reserved

Printed in the United States of America

5 4 3 2 1

Library of Congress Cataloging-in-Publication Data

Harvard business review on advancing your career.
    p. cm. — (Harvard business review paperback)
    ISBN 978-1-4221-7223-0 (alk. paper)
  1. Career development. 2. Promotions. I. Harvard business review.
    HF5381.H277 2011
    650.14—dc22

                                                      2011000137

Contents

Harvard Business Review

on

ADVANCING YOUR CAREER

How Will You Measure Your Life?

by Clayton M. Christensen

BEFORE I PUBLISHED *The Innovator's Dilemma,* I got a call from Andrew Grove, then the chairman of Intel. He had read one of my early papers about disruptive technology, and he asked if I could talk to his direct reports and explain my research and what it implied for Intel. Excited, I flew to Silicon Valley and showed up at the appointed time, only to have Grove say, "Look, stuff has happened. We have only 10 minutes for you. Tell us what your model of disruption means for Intel." I said that I couldn't—that I needed a full 30 minutes to explain the model, because only with it as context would any comments about Intel make sense. Ten minutes into my explanation, Grove interrupted: "Look, I've got your model. Just tell us what it means for Intel."

I insisted that I needed 10 more minutes to describe how the process of disruption had worked its way through a very different industry, steel, so that he and his team could understand how disruption worked. I told the story of how Nucor and other steel minimills had begun by attacking the lowest end of the market—steel reinforcing bars, or rebar—and later moved up toward the high end, undercutting the traditional steel mills.

When I finished the minimill story, Grove said, "OK, I get it. What it means for Intel is …," and then went on to articulate what would become the company's strategy for going to the bottom of the market to launch the Celeron processor.

I've thought about that a million times since. If I had been suckered into telling Andy Grove what he should think about the microprocessor business, I'd have been killed. But instead of telling him what to think, I taught him how to think—and then he reached what I felt was the correct decision on his own.

That experience had a profound influence on me. When people ask what I think they should do, I rarely answer their question directly. Instead, I run the question aloud through one of my models. I'll describe how the process in the model worked its way through an industry quite different from their own. And then, more often than not, they'll say, "OK, I get it." And they'll answer their own question more insightfully than I could have.

My class at HBS is structured to help my students understand what good management theory is and how it is built. To that backbone I attach different models or theories that help students think about the various dimensions of a general manager's job in stimulating

Idea in Brief

Harvard Business School's Christensen teaches aspiring MBAs how to apply management and innovation theories to build stronger companies. But he also believes that these models can help people lead better lives. In this article, he explains how, exploring questions everyone needs to ask. How can I be happy in my career? How can I be sure that my relationship with my family is an enduring source of happiness? And how can I live my life with integrity? The answer to the first question comes from Frederick Herzberg's assertion that the most powerful motivator isn't money; it's the opportunity to learn, grow in responsibilities, contribute, and be recognized. That's why management, if practiced well, can be the noblest of occupations; no others offer as many ways to help people find those opportunities. It isn't about buying, selling, and investing in companies, as many think. The principles of resource allocation can help people attain happiness at home. If not managed masterfully, what emerges from a firm's resource allocation process can be very different from the strategy management intended to follow. That's true in life too: If you're not guided by a clear sense of purpose, you're likely to fritter away your time and energy on obtaining the most tangible, short-term signs of achievement, not what's really important to you. And just as a focus on marginal costs can cause bad corporate decisions, it can lead people astray. The marginal cost of doing something wrong "just this once" always seems alluringly low. You don't see the end result to which that path leads. The key is to define what you stand for and draw the line in a safe place.

innovation and growth. In each session we look at one company through the lenses of those theories—using them to explain how the company got into its situation and to examine what managerial actions will yield the needed results.

On the last day of class, I ask my students to turn those theoretical lenses on themselves, to find cogent answers to three questions: First, how can I be sure that I'll be happy in my career? Second, how can I be sure that my relationships with my spouse and my family become an enduring source of happiness? Third, how can I be sure I'll stay out of jail? Though the last question sounds lighthearted, it's not. Two of the 32 people in my Rhodes scholar class spent time in jail. Jeff Skilling of Enron fame was a classmate of mine at HBS. These were good guys—but something in their lives sent them off in the wrong direction.

As the students discuss the answers to these questions, I open my own life to them as a case study of sorts, to illustrate how they can use the theories from our course to guide their life decisions.

One of the theories that gives great insight on the first question—how to be sure we find happiness in our careers—is from Frederick Herzberg, who asserts that the powerful motivator in our lives isn't money; it's the opportunity to learn, grow in responsibilities, contribute to others, and be recognized for achievements. I tell the students about a vision of sorts I had while I was running the company I founded before becoming an academic. In my mind's eye I saw one of my managers leave for work one morning with a relatively strong level of self-esteem. Then I pictured her driving home to her family 10 hours later, feeling unappreciated, frustrated, underutilized, and demeaned. I imagined how profoundly her lowered self-esteem affected the way she interacted with her children. The vision in my mind then fast-forwarded to another day, when she drove home with greater self-esteem—feeling that she had learned a lot, been recognized for achieving valuable things, and played a significant role in the success of some important initiatives. I then imagined how positively that affected her as a spouse and a parent. My conclusion: Management is the most noble of professions if it's practiced well. No other occupation offers as many ways to help others learn and grow, take responsibility and be recognized for achievement, and contribute to the success of a team. More and more MBA students come to school thinking that a career in business means buying, selling, and investing in companies. That's unfortunate. Doing deals doesn't yield the deep rewards that come from building up people.

I want students to leave my classroom knowing that.

Create a Strategy for Your Life

A theory that is helpful in answering the second question—How can I ensure that my relationship with my family proves to be an enduring source of happiness?—concerns how strategy is defined and implemented. Its primary insight is that a company's strategy is determined by the types of initiatives that management invests in. If a company's resource allocation process is not managed masterfully, what emerges from it can be very different from what management intended. Because companies' decision-making systems are designed to steer investments to initiatives that offer the most tangible and immediate returns, companies shortchange investments in initiatives that are crucial to their long-term strategies.

The Class of 2010

"**I CAME TO BUSINESS SCHOOL** knowing exactly what I wanted to do—and I'm leaving choosing the exact opposite. I've worked in the private sector all my life, because everyone always told me that's where smart people are. But I've decided to try government and see if I can find more meaning there.

"I used to think that industry was very safe. The recession has shown us that nothing is safe."

Ruhana Hafiz, Harvard Business School, Class of 2010
Her Plans: To join the FBI as a special adviser (a management track position)

"You could see a shift happening at HBS. Money used to be number one in the job search. When you make a ton of money, you want more of it. Ironic thing. You start to forget what the drivers of happiness are and what things are really important. A lot of people on campus see money differently now. They think, 'What's the minimum I need to have, and what else drives my life?' instead of 'What's the place where I can get the maximum of both?'"

Patrick Chun, Harvard Business School, Class of 2010
His Plans: To join Bain Capital

"The financial crisis helped me realize that you have to do what you really love in life. My current vision of success is based on the

---

Over the years I've watched the fates of my HBS classmates from 1979 unfold; I've seen more and more of them come to reunions unhappy, divorced, and alienated from their children. I can guarantee you that not a single one of them graduated with the deliberate strategy of getting divorced and raising children who would become estranged from them. And yet a shocking number of them impact I can have, the experiences I can gain, and the happiness I can find personally, much more so than the pursuit of money or prestige. My main motivations are (1) to be with my family and people I care about; (2) to do something fun, exciting, and impactful; and (3) to pursue a long-term career in entrepreneurship, where I can build companies that change the way the world works."

Matt Salzberg, Harvard Business School, Class of 2010
His Plans: To work for Bessemer Venture Partners

"Because I'm returning to McKinsey, it probably seems like not all that much has changed for me. But while I was at HBS, I decided to do the dual degree at the Kennedy School. With the elections in 2008 and the economy looking shaky, it seemed more compelling for me to get a better understanding of the public and nonprofit sectors. In a way, that drove my return to McKinsey, where I'll have the ability to explore private, public, and nonprofit sectors.

"The recession has made us step back and take stock of how lucky we are. The crisis to us is 'Are we going to have a job by April?' Crisis to a lot of people is 'Are we going to stay in our home?'"

John Coleman, Harvard Business School, Class of 2010
His Plans: To return to McKinsey & Company

implemented that strategy. The reason? They didn't keep the purpose of their lives front and center as they decided how to spend their time, talents, and energy.

It's quite startling that a significant fraction of the 900 students that HBS draws each year from the world's best have given little thought to the purpose of their lives. I tell the students that HBS might be one of their last chances to reflect deeply on that question. If they think that they'll have more time and energy to reflect later, they're nuts, because life only gets more demanding: You take on a mortgage; you're working 70 hours a week; you have a spouse and children.

For me, having a clear purpose in my life has been essential. But it was something I had to think long and hard about before I understood it. When I was a Rhodes scholar, I was in a very demanding academic program, trying to cram an extra year's worth of work into my time at Oxford. I decided to spend an hour every night reading, thinking, and praying about why God put me on this earth. That was a very challenging commitment to keep, because every hour I spent doing that, I wasn't studying applied econometrics. I was conflicted about whether I could really afford to take that time away from my studies, but I stuck with it—and ultimately figured out the purpose of my life.

Had I instead spent that hour each day learning the latest techniques for mastering the problems of autocorrelation in regression analysis, I would have badly misspent my life. I apply the tools of econometrics a few times a year, but I apply my knowledge of the purpose of my life every day. It's the single most useful thing I've ever learned. I promise my students that if they take the time to figure out their life purpose, they'll look back on it as the most important thing they discovered at HBS. If they don't figure it out, they will just sail off without a rudder and get buffeted in the very rough seas of life. Clarity about their purpose will trump knowledge of activity-based costing, balanced scorecards, core competence, disruptive innovation, the four Ps, and the five forces.

My purpose grew out of my religious faith, but faith isn't the only thing that gives people direction. For example, one of my former students decided that his purpose was to bring honesty and economic prosperity to his country and to raise children who were as capably committed to this cause, and to each other, as he was. His purpose is focused on family and others—as mine is.

The choice and successful pursuit of a profession is but one tool for achieving your purpose. But without a purpose, life can become hollow.

Allocate Your Resources

Your decisions about allocating your personal time, energy, and talent ultimately shape your life's strategy.

I have a bunch of "businesses" that compete for these resources: I'm trying to have a rewarding relationship with my wife, raise great kids, contribute to my community, succeed in my career, contribute to my church, and so on. And I have exactly the same problem that a corporation does. I have a limited amount of time and energy and talent. How much do I devote to each of these pursuits?

Allocation choices can make your life turn out to be very different from what you intended. Sometimes that's good: Opportunities that you never planned for emerge. But if you misinvest your resources, the outcome can be bad. As I think about my former classmates who inadvertently invested for lives of hollow unhappiness, I can't help believing that their troubles relate right back to a short-term perspective.

When people who have a high need for achievement—and that includes all Harvard Business School graduates—have an extra half hour of time or an extra ounce of energy, they'll unconsciously allocate it to activities that yield the most tangible accomplishments. And our careers provide the most concrete evidence that we're moving forward. You ship a product, finish a design, complete a presentation, close a sale, teach a class, publish a paper, get paid, get promoted. In contrast, investing time and energy in your relationship with your spouse and children typically doesn't offer that same immediate sense of achievement. Kids misbehave every day. It's really not until 20 years down the road that you can put your hands on your hips and say, "I raised a good son or a good daughter." You can neglect your relationship with your spouse, and on a day-to-day basis, it doesn't seem as if things are deteriorating. People who are driven to excel have this unconscious propensity to underinvest in their families and overinvest in their careers—even though intimate and loving relationships with their families are the most powerful and enduring source of happiness.

If you study the root causes of business disasters, over and over you'll find this predisposition toward endeavors that offer immediate gratification. If you look at personal lives through that lens, you'll see the same stunning and sobering pattern: people allocating fewer and fewer resources to the things they would have once said mattered most.

Create a Culture

There's an important model in our class called the Tools of Cooperation, which basically says that being a visionary manager isn't all it's cracked up to be. It's one thing to see into the foggy future with acuity and chart the course corrections that the company must make. But it's quite another to persuade employees who might not see the changes ahead to line up and work cooperatively to take the company in that new direction. Knowing what tools to wield to elicit the needed cooperation is a critical managerial skill.

The theory arrays these tools along two dimensions— the extent to which members of the organization agree on what they want from their participation in the enterprise, and the extent to which they agree on what actions will produce the desired results. When there is little agreement on both axes, you have to use "power tools"—coercion, threats, punishment, and so on—to secure cooperation. Many companies start in this quadrant, which is why the founding executive team must play such an assertive role in defining what must be done and how. If employees' ways of working together to address those tasks succeed over and over, consensus begins to form. MIT's Edgar Schein has described this process as the mechanism by which a culture is built. Ultimately, people don't even think about whether their way of doing things yields success. They embrace priorities andfollow procedures by instinct and assumption rather than by explicit decision—which means that they've created a culture. Culture, in compelling but unspoken ways, dictates the proven, acceptable methods by which members of the group address recurrent problems. And culture defines the priority given to different types of problems. It can be a powerful management tool.

In using this model to address the question, How can I be sure that my family becomes an enduring source of happiness?, my students quickly see that the simplest tools that parents can wield to elicit cooperation from children are power tools. But there comes a point during the teen years when power tools no longer work. At that point parents start wishing that they had begun working with their children at a very young age to build a culture at home in which children instinctively behave respectfully toward one another, obey their parents, and choose the right thing to do. Families have cultures, just as companies do. Those cultures can be built consciously or evolve inadvertently.

If you want your kids to have strong self-esteem and confidence that they can solve hard problems, those qualities won't magically materialize in high school. You have to design them into your family's culture— and you have to think about this very early on. Like employees, children build self-esteem by doing things that are hard and learning what works.

Avoid the "Marginal Costs" Mistake

We're taught in finance and economics that in evaluating alternative investments, we should ignore sunk and fixed costs, and instead base decisions on the marginal costs and marginal revenues that each alternative entails. We learn in our course that this doctrine biases companies to leverage what they have put in place to succeed in the past, instead of guiding them to create the capabilities they'll need in the future. If we knew the future would be exactly the same as the past, that approach would be fine. But if the future's different—and it almost always is—then it's the wrong thing to do.

This theory addresses the third question I discuss with my students—how to live a life of integrity (stay out of jail). Unconsciously, we often employ the marginal cost doctrine in our personal lives when we choose between right and wrong. A voice in our head says, "Look, I know that as a general rule, most people shouldn't do this. But in this particular extenuating circumstance, just this once, it's OK." The marginal cost of doing something wrong "just this once" always seems alluringly low. It suckers you in, and you don't ever look at where that path ultimately is headed and at the full costs that the choice entails. Justification for infidelity and dishonesty in all their manifestations lies in the marginal cost economics of "just this once."

I'd like to share a story about how I came to understand the potential damage of "just this once" in my own life. I played on the Oxford University varsity basketball team. We worked our tails off and finished the season undefeated. The guys on the team were the best friends I've ever had in my life. We got to the

British equivalent of the NCAA tournament—and made it to the final four. It turned out the championship game was scheduled to be played on a Sunday. I had made a personal commitment to God at age 16 that I would never play ball on Sunday. So I went to the coach and explained my problem. He was incredulous. My teammates were, too, because I was the starting center. Every one of the guys on the team came to me and said, "You've got to play. Can't you break the rule just this one time?"

I'm a deeply religious man, so I went away and prayed about what I should do. I got a very clear feeling that I shouldn't break my commitment—so I didn't play in the championship game.

In many ways that was a small decision—involving one of several thousand Sundays in my life. In theory, surely I could have crossed over the line just that one time and then not done it again. But looking back on it, resisting the temptation whose logic was "In this extenuating circumstance, just this once, it's OK" has proven to be one of the most important decisions of my life. Why? My life has been one unending stream of extenuating circumstances. Had I crossed the line that one time, I would have done it over and over in the years that followed.

The lesson I learned from this is that it's easier to hold to your principles 100% of the time than it is to hold to them 98% of the time. If you give in to "just this once," based on a marginal cost analysis, as some of my former classmates have done, you'll regret where you end up. You've got to define for yourself what you stand for and draw the line in a safe place.

Remember the Importance of Humility

I got this insight when I was asked to teach a class on humility at Harvard College. I asked all the students to describe the most humble person they knew. One characteristic of these humble people stood out: They had a high level of self-esteem. They knew who they were, and they felt good about who they were. We also decided that humility was defined not by self-deprecating behavior or attitudes but by the esteem with which you regard others. Good behavior flows naturally from that kind of humility. For example, you would never steal from someone, because you respect that person too much. You'd never lie to someone, either.

It's crucial to take a sense of humility into the world. By the time you make it to a top graduate school, almost all your learning has come from people who are smarter and more experienced than you: parents, teachers, bosses. But once you've finished at Harvard Business School or any other top academic institution, the vast majority of people you'll interact with on a day-to-day basis may not be smarter than you. And if your attitude is that only smarter people have something to teach you, your learning opportunities will be very limited. But if you have a humble eagerness to learn something from everybody, your learning opportunities will be unlimited. Generally, you can be humble only if you feel really good about yourself—and you want to help those around you feel really good about themselves, too. When we see people acting in an abusive, arrogant, or demeaning manner toward others, their behavior almost always is a symptom of their lack of self-esteem. They need to put someone else down to feel good about themselves.

Choose the Right Yardstick

This past year I was diagnosed with cancer and faced the possibility that my life would end sooner than I'd planned. Thankfully, it now looks as if I'll be spared. But the experience has given me important insight into my life.

I have a pretty clear idea of how my ideas have generated enormous revenue for companies that have used my research; I know I've had a substantial impact. But as I've confronted this disease, it's been interesting to see how unimportant that impact is to me now. I've concluded that the metric by which God will assess my life isn't dollars but the individual people whose lives I've touched.

I think that's the way it will work for us all. Don't worry about the level of individual prominence you have achieved; worry about the individuals you have helped become better people. This is my final recommendation: Think about the metric by which your life will be judged, and make a resolution to live every day so that in the end, your life will be judged a success.

CLAYTON M. CHRISTENSEN is the Robert and Jane Cizik Professor of Business Administration at Harvard Business School.

Originally published in July 2010. Reprint R1007B

Turn the Job You Have into the Job You Want

by Amy Wrzesniewski, Justin M. Berg, and Jane E. Dutton

A 30-YEAR-OLD MIDLEVEL MANAGER—let's call her Fatima—is struggling at work, but you wouldn't know it from outward appearances. A star member of her team in the marketing division of a large multinational foods company, Fatima consistently hits her benchmarks and goals. She invests long hours and has built relationships with colleagues that she deeply values. And her senior managers think of her as one of the company's high potentials.

But outside the office, Fatima (who asked not to be identified by her real name) would admit that she feels stagnant in her job, trapped by the tension between day-to-day demands and what she really wants to be doing: exploring how the company can use social media in its marketing efforts. Twitter, her cause-marketing blog, and mobile gadgets are her main passions. She'd like to look for another job, but given the slow recovery from the recession, sticking it out seems like her best (and perhaps only) option. "I'm still working hard," she tells a friend. "But I'm stuck. Every week, I feel less and less motivated. I'm beginning to wonder why I wanted this position in the first place."

Sound familiar? Over the past several years, we've spoken with hundreds of people, in a variety of industries and occupations, who, like Fatima, are feeling stuck—that dreaded word again. According to a recent survey of 5,000 U.S. households by The Conference Board, only 45% of those polled say they are satisfied with their jobs—down from about 60% in 1987, the first year the survey was conducted.

If you're in this situation, and changing roles or companies is unrealistic given the tough economy, what can you do? A growing body of research suggests that an exercise we call "job crafting" can be a powerful tool for reenergizing and reimagining your work life. It involves redefining your job to incorporate your motives, strengths, and passions. The exercise prompts you to visualize the job, map its elements, and reorganize them to better suit you. In this way, you can put personal touches on how you see and do your job, and you'll gain a greater sense of control at work—which is especially critical at a time when you're probably working longer and harder and expecting to retire later. Perhaps job crafting's best feature is that it's driven by you, not your supervisor.

This exercise involves assessing and then altering one or more of the following core aspects of work.

Idea in Brief

If you're unhappy at work, and changing roles or companies may be unrealistic given the tough economy, what can you do? A growing body of research suggests that a process called job crafting can be a powerful tool for reenergizing and reimagining your life at work. It involves redefining your current job description to better incorporate your motives, strengths, and passions. The exercise prompts you to visualize your job graphically, map its elements, and reorganize them to shape the job to better suit you. In this way, you can put your own personal touches on the way you see and do your job; and you'll gain a greater sense of control at work—all of which is especially critical at a time when you're probably working longer and

harder and will be retiring later. Perhaps job crafting's best feature is that it's driven by you, not your supervisor. Research with a range of organizations indicates that employees who engage in job crafting often end up more engaged and satisfied with their work lives, achieve higher levels of performance in their organizations, and report greater personal resilience. And organizations have a lot to gain by enabling job crafting: The exercise lets managers turn the reins over to employees, empowering them to become "job entrepreneurs." And when pay resources are constrained or promotions impossible, job crafting may give companies a different way to motivate and retain their most talented employees.

Tasks

You can change the boundaries of your job by taking on more or fewer tasks, expanding or diminishing their scope, or changing how they are performed. A sales manager, for instance, might take on additional event planning because he likes the challenge of organizing people and logistics.

Relationships

You can change the nature or extent of your interactions with other people. A managing director, for example, might create mentoring relationships with young associates as a way to connect with and teach those who represent the future of the firm.

Perceptions

You can change how you think about the purpose of certain aspects of your job; or you can reframe the job as a whole. The director of a nonprofit institution, for instance, might choose to think of his job as two separate parts, one not particularly enjoyable (the pursuit of contributions and grants) and one very meaningful (creating opportunities for emerging artists). Or the leader of an R&D unit might come to see her work as a way of advancing the science in her field rather than simply managing projects.

Our research with a range of organizations—from *Fortune* 500 companies to small nonprofits—indicates that employees (at all levels, in all kinds of occupations) who try job crafting often end up more engaged and satisfied with their work lives, achieve higher levels of performance in their organizations, and report greater personal resilience.

For their part, organizations have a lot to gain by enabling job crafting. Most job-redesign models put the onus on managers to help employees find satisfaction in their work; in reality, leaders rarely have sufficient time to devote to this process. Job crafting lets managers turn the reins over to employees, empowering them to become "job entrepreneurs." And when pay resources are constrained or promotions impossible, job crafting may give companies a different way to motivate and retain their most talented employees. It can even help transform poor performers.

Despite these benefits, however, job crafting can be easy to overlook: Time pressures and other constraints may compel you to see your job as a fixed list of duties. Or you may be afraid of getting mired in office politics, stepping on other people's toes simply because you're unhappy at work. Job crafting requires—and ultimately engenders—a different mind-set, however: Your job comprises a set of building blocks that you can reconfigure to create more engaging and fulfilling experiences at work.

Diagramming Your Job

Back at the multinational foods company, Fatima is still frustrated. What would happen if she engaged in job crafting? She's already been reflecting on her dissatisfaction, albeit in no systematic way. Job crafting would give her the means to diagram a more ideal—but still realistic—version of her job, one better aligned with her motives, strengths, and passions.

First, she looks at the present makeup of her job. In her "before diagram," Fatima uses a series of squares to represent the tasks that her job comprises, with larger squares representing time-intensive tasks, and smaller squares tasks to which she devotes less time. (See the exhibit "Fatima's before diagram.")

She notices that she's spending lots of time monitoring her team's performance, answering questions, and directing market research. She's spending a fair number of hours setting budgets, writing reports, and running meetings. And she's spending very little time on critical tasks such as professional development and designing marketing strategies. These tasks are in the smallest

Fatima's before diagram

Once she has created her before diagram, this midlevel marketing manager immediately sees that she's spending lots of time on tasks that don't engage her passions—for instance, monitoring her team's performance, answering questions, and directing market research— and much less on tasks that are meaningful to her.

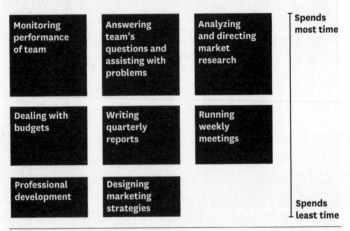

Monitoring performance of team	Answering team's questions and assisting with problems	Analyzing and directing market research	⌐ Spends most time
Dealing with budgets	Writing quarterly reports	Running weekly meetings	
Professional development	Designing marketing strategies		Spends least time

squares. Looking at the full sweep of her job in this way gives Fatima a clear sense—truly at a glance—of exactly where she is devoting her time and energy.

Next, she concentrates on changes that would increase her engagement at work. This "after diagram" will serve as the visual plan for her future. (See the exhibit "Fatima's after diagram.")

Fatima's after diagram

In Fatima's after diagram, it's easier to see how she can connect her tasks to her motives, strengths, and passions. For instance, one of her motives is to cultivate meaningful relationships and achieve personal growth. Her strengths include her one-on-one communication skills and technical savvy. And among her passions are teaching others and using and learning about new technology.

In this after diagram, the sizes of the blocks represent a better al-location of Fatima's time, energy, and attention. The borders around groups of tasks suggest the common purpose they serve. By rearrang-ing the shapes on the page, Fatima gains a greater appreciation for how the different elements of her job come together.

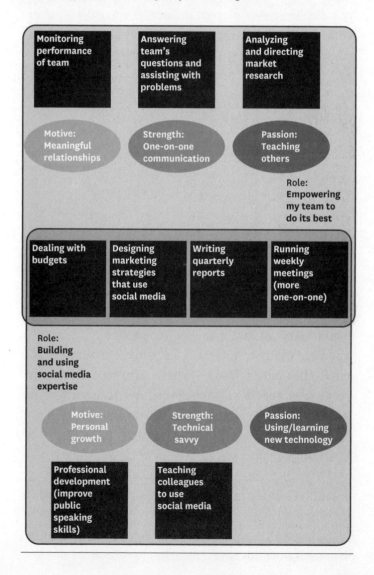

She begins by identifying her motives, strengths, and passions—three important considerations in determining which aspects of her job will keep her engaged and inspire higher performance. Each will be represented by a different shade of gray. Her main motives, for instance, are cultivating meaningful relationships and achieving personal growth. She plugs these into light gray ovals. Fatima takes stock of her core strengths: one-on-one communication and technical savvy. These appear in the medium gray ovals. And she highlights her passions: teaching others and using and learning new technology—entered in dark gray ovals.

Then, using her before diagram as a frame of reference, Fatima creates a new set of task blocks whose size represents a better allocation of her time, energy, and attention. To take advantage of how well "designing marketing strategies" suits her motives, strengths, and passions, she not only moves it from a small to a medium block but also add "use social media" to this newly expanded task. To incorporate even more social media into her job, she adds a small task block to represent "teaching colleagues to use social media." And for those tasks that do not fit her as well, she makes a note to adapt them (for instance, using "professional development" to "improve public speaking skills").

She draws rectangles around groups of tasks that she thinks serve a common purpose or role. For example, she identifies "building and using social media expertise" as one role. Framing her roles in this way is meaningful to her because it taps into her key strengths and passions. By rearranging the shapes, Fatima gains a greater appreciation for how the elements of her job come together.

A New Outlook

Fatima then moves to the final step of the exercise, in which she considers the challenges she will probably face in making her new job configuration a reality. She would like to use her technical savvy to help other marketing teams and departments take advantage of social media, but she is concerned about encroaching on their work or insulting them by offering her expertise. With her after diagram in hand, Fatima takes another look at the list of projects sitting in her in-box and begins to consider how to incorporate social media into them.

Tasks

She identifies two possibilities: a new snack food aimed at teens and a cross-company initiative to improve communication between Marketing and Sales. Fatima thinks a campaign involving Facebook and Twitter could help build buzz around the snack food—and reveal to the organization the benefits and limitations of reaching out to a new demographic. And by launching a blog, Fatima and her colleagues in Marketing could track initiatives and communications from members of the Sales division.

Relationships

Fatima recognizes, of course, that she'll need support to establish the technological presence she envisions for these two projects. She must build or refocus her ties to others in the company in order to learn about the best ways to move forward. She recalls that Steve Porter is constantly fiddling with the latest gadgets in weekly interdepartmental meetings and that he is known for the clever ways he uses social media to keep salespeople in the loop. She decides to approach him for help. Within a month, Steve's and her own employees' support has unleashed a wave of interest in and knowledge about how to put technology closer to the heart of the division's work. Her initiatives have become testing grounds for using social media to accomplish other important goals. Fatima has been recognized as the driver of these programs and finds that managers from other divisions are coming to her to learn more about how they might use her ideas in their own projects—all of which is encouraging her to be bolder in introducing new ideas and technology.

Perceptions

Rather than thinking of her work as a daily slog, she begins to see herself as an innovator at the intersection of marketing and technology. And she views herself as an entrepreneurial pioneer unafraid of experiments that could bridge those worlds. She also, to her pleasure, recognizes that rather than taking her away from her prescribed goals, her passion for deploying technology in pursuit of these objectives gives her a more fulfilling way to approach them.

Ivan's Story

In another company, in another part of the world, Ivan Carter is caught between a rock and a hard place. But the source of angst for this 45-year-old operations manager at a global office products company is quite different from Fatima's. He's a solid B player with a dedicated and successful team. Ivan leads a group that serves Latin America, and he reports to both the head of global operations and the head of the Latin America group. His relationship with the latter is great, but the operations head is often nonresponsive or even hostile when Ivan needs information or support. All his efforts to strengthen the relationship have been met with silence. He likes his job, but he often leaves the office with his stomach in knots.

Ivan knows he can either accept the reality of his toxic relationship with the head of operations or change his situation. So, during his next phone meeting with the head of Latin America, he pushes a bit to explore what interests her most about the role of the operations group in that region. She sees the group as becoming more critical for cost savings as economic recovery drags on—a major focus for the CEO, as well. Ivan spots an opportunity. He can build on what is already a good relationship by directing more of his efforts to special projects that will save money in that region. Sensing a chance to craft his job, Ivan focuses more and more of his time and energy on this aspect of his work, which wins him exposure and credit as the projects he takes on create significant savings for the company. As a bonus, he spends more time interacting with the Latin America head while meeting his responsibilities to the operations head without having to interact with him as much. After several months, Ivan learns that the Latin America head has recommended him highly to others in the C-suite.

Fatima focused first on tasks and then on relationships. By centering his job crafting primarily on relationships (the ones that energized rather then depleted him), Ivan was able to figure out how to change his job for the better.

The Limits of Job Crafting

Not all job crafting is beneficial. It can be stressful if as a result you take on too much or alter tasks without understanding your manager's goals. Since job crafting is something you can do on your own, it's important to be open about the process. Your manager may even be able to help you identify opportunities for redistributing tasks in complementary ways. After all, one person's dreaded assignment may be another's favorite.

To win others' support for your job crafting, do these three things:

- Focus on deploying an individual or organizational strength that will create value for others. For instance, Fatima positioned her work to enhance what other teams were doing, while Ivan found a way to help meet the objectives of the Latin America group.

- Build trust with others (typically your supervisor). Fatima assured her supervisor that she wouldn't let tasks slide and that some of her newer tasks could become central to the organization. Ivan was careful to align his efforts with his role, building trust with the head of the Latin America group.

- Direct your job-crafting efforts toward the people who are most likely to accommodate you. Fatima reached out to Steve Porter because he was interested in her plans to bring technology into the heart of her job tasks. Ivan realized that his time would be wasted pursuing a toxic relationship and instead focused on a more promising one.

Job crafting is a simple visual framework that can help you make meaningful and lasting changes in your job-in good economies and bad. But it all has to start with taking a step back from the daily grind and realizing that you actually have the ability to reconfigure the elements of your work.

The bottom line? Make sure that you are shaping your job, not letting your job shape you.

AMY WRZESNIEWSKI is an associate professor of organizational behavior at the Yale School of Management. **JUSTIN M. BERG** is a doctoral student at the University of Pennsylvania's Wharton School. **JANE E. DUTTON** is the Robert L. Kahn Distinguished University Professor of Business Administration and Psychology at the University of Michigan's Ross School of Business.

Originally published in June 2010. Reprint R1006K

How to Stay Stuck in the Wrong Career

by Herminia Ibarra

EVERYONE KNOWS A STORY about a smart and talented businessperson who has lost his or her passion for work, who no longer looks forward to going to the office yet remains stuck without a visible way out. Most everyone knows a story, too, about a person who ditched a 20-year career to pursue something completely different—the lawyer who gave it all up to become a writer or the auditor who quit her accounting firm to start her own toy company—and is the happier for it.

"Am I doing what is right for me, or should I change direction?" is one of the most pressing questions in the mid-career professional's mind today. The numbers of people making major career changes, not to mention those just thinking about it, have risen significantly over the last decade and continue to grow. But the difference between the person who yearns for change yet stays put and the person who takes the leap to find re-newed fulfillment at midcareer is not what you might expect. Consider the following examples.

Susan Fontaine made a clean break with her unfulfill-ing past as partner and head of the strategy practice at a top consulting firm. But the former management consultant—her name, like the names of the other people I studied, has been changed for this article—had not yet had the time to figure out a future direction. When a close client offered her the top strategy job at a *Financial Times* 100 firm, she took it. She was ready for change, and the opportunity was too good to pass up. To her dismay, this position—though perfect according to what she calls "the relentless logic of a post-MBA CV"—was no different from her old job in all the aspects she had been seeking to change. Two weeks into the new role, she realized she had made a terrible mistake.

After a four-week executive education program at a top business school, Harris Roberts, a regulatory affairs director at a major health care firm, was ready for change. He wanted bottom-line responsibility, and he itched to put into practice some of the cutting-edge ideas he had learned in the program. His long-time mentor, the company's CEO, had promised, "When you come back, we'll give you a business unit." But upon Harris's return, a complicated new product intro-duction delayed the long-awaited transition. He was needed in his old role, so he was asked to postpone his dream. As always, Harris put the company first. But he was disappointed; there was no challenge anymore. Resigned to waiting it out, he created for himself a

Idea in Brief

Are you one of the growing number of people struggling to make mid-career changes? Searching for ten easy steps to professional reinvention? Or awaiting flashes of insight—while opportunities pass you by?

Would you be willing to jettison all you've heard about career transition and follow a crooked path—rather than the straight and narrow one that's gotten you nowhere?

If so, consider the counterintuitive approach described in this article. It'll have you *doing* instead of infinitely planning. Taking *action* instead of endless self-assessment tests. You'll reinvent your **working identity**—your sense of who you are as a professional—by experimenting with who you *could* be.

"network of mentors," senior members of the firm whom he enlisted to guide his development and help him try to land the coveted general management role. Eighteen months later, he was still doing essentially the same job.

A milestone birthday, upheaval in his personal life, and a negative performance evaluation—the first of his career—combined to make a "snapping point" for Gary McCarthy. After business school, the former investment banker and consultant had taken a job at a blue-chip firm by default, biding his time until he found his "true passion." Now, he decided, it was time to make a proactive career choice. Determined to get it right, Gary did all the correct things. He started with a career psychologist who gave him a battery of tests to help him figure out his work interests and values. He talked to headhunters, friends, and family and read best-selling books on career change. By his own account, none of the

Idea in Practice

Sounds Reasonable, But . . .

Consider the traditional "plan and implement" approach to career change: Assess your interests, skills, and experience; identify appropriate jobs; consult friends, colleagues, career counselors; take the plunge.

This all *sounds* reasonable— but it actually fosters stagnation. You get mired in introspection while searching for your "one true self" a futile quest, since individuals have many possible selves. Your ideal won't necessarily find a match in the real world. Worse, this method encourages making a big change all at once—which can land you in the wrong job.

Sounds Crazy, But . . .

Now consider the "test and learn" method: You put *several* working identities into practice, refining them until they're sufficiently grounded in experience to inspire more decisive steps. You make your possible *future* working identities vivid, tangible, and compelling—countering the tendency to grab familiar work when the unknown becomes too scary.

Reinventing your working identity takes several years— and may land you in surprising places. But that doesn't mean the process must be random. These tactics provide a method to the seeming madness:

- **Craft experiments.** Play with new professional roles on a limited but tangible scale, without compromising your current job. Try freelance assignments or pro bono work. Moonlight. Use sabbaticals or

advice was very useful. He researched possible industries and companies. He made two lists: completely different professions involving things he was passionate about and variations on what he was already doing. A year later, a viable alternative had yet to materialize.

When I consider the experiences of these people and dozens of others I have studied over the past few years, there can be no doubt: Despite the rhetoric, a true extended vacations to explore new directions.

Example: A former investment banker dabbled in wine tours and scuba diving businesses before determining that such work wouldn't hold his interest long-term. Realizing a "more normal" career path would better serve his emotional and financial needs, he is now a internal venture capitalist for a media company.

- **Shift connections.** Strangers can best help you see who you're becoming, providing fresh ideas uncolored by your previous identity. Make new connections by working for people you've long admired and can learn from. Find people— perhaps through alumni and company networks—who can help you grow into your possible new selves.

- **Make sense.** Infuse events with special meaning. Weave them into a story about who you're becoming. Relate that story publicly. You'll clarify your intentions, stay motivated, and inspire others' support.

Example: An investment banker considering fiction writing visited an astrologer, who noted that forces pulling him in opposing directions (stability versus creative expression) were irreconcilable. He told everyone this story and wrote about it in his local newspaper. The more he communicated it, the more the incident made sense— and the more friends and family supported his writing ambitions.

change of direction is very hard to swing. This isn't because managers or professionals are typically unwilling to change; on the contrary, many make serious attempts to reinvent themselves, devoting large amounts of time and energy to the process at great professional and personal risk. But despite heroic efforts, they remain stuck in the wrong careers, not living up to their potential and sacrificing professional fulfillment.

Studying Career Change

CERTAIN CAREER TRANSITIONS have been thoroughly studied and are well understood: a move into a position of greater managerial responsibility and organizational status, a transfer to a similar job in a new company or industry, a lateral move into a different work function within a familiar field. But few researchers have investigated how managers and professionals go about making a true change of direction.

My research is an in-depth study of 39 people who changed, or were in the process of trying to change, careers. Determining the magnitude of any work transition is highly subjective. Who, apart from the person who has lived through it, can say whether a shift is radical or incremental? After interviewing dozens of people who were making very different kinds of career moves, I settled on a three-part definition of career change.

Some of the people in my study made significant changes in the context in which they worked, most typically jumping from large, established companies to small, entrepreneurial organizations or to self-employment or between the for-profit and nonprofit sectors. Others made major changes in the content of the work, sometimes leaving occupations, such as medicine, law or academia, that they had trained for extensively. The majority made significant changes in both what they did and where they did it, but most important, all experienced a feeling

Many academics and career counselors observe this inertia and conclude that the problem lies in basic human motives: We fear change, lack readiness, are unwilling to make sacrifices, sabotage ourselves. My in-depth research (see the sidebar "Studying Career Change" for an explanation of my methods) leads me to a different conclusion: People most often fail because they go about it all wrong. Indeed, the conventional of having reached a crossroad, one that would require psychological change.

My sample ranged in age from 32 to 51, with an average of 41. I chose this range not to coincide with the infamous midlife crisis but to study a group of people with enough experience in one career to make a shift to another high-stakes endeavor. Sixty-five percent of the participants were men. Almost half of the subjects lived and worked outside the United States, mostly in France and the UK. It was a highly credentialed sample: All had college degrees, and about three-fourths held graduate or professional degrees (business, science, law, and so on). They represented all walks of managerial and professional life, including business management, law, finance, academia, medicine, science, and technology.

Some of the interviews were retrospective, with people who had already completed their changes. With people at earlier stages of the transition, I conducted an average of three interviews over two to three years. The interviews were open-ended, typically beginning with: "Tell me about your career to date." Between the interviews, I had e-mail exchanges and telephone conversations with participants to keep track of their progress. I supplemented this core study with many shorter interviews involving a range of career change professionals, including headhunters, venture capitalists, career counselors, and outplacement specialists.

wisdom on how to change careers is in fact a prescription for how to stay put. The problem lies in our methods, not our motives.

In my study, I saw many people try a conventional approach and then languish for months, if not years. But by taking a different tack, one I came to call the practice of *working identity,* they eventually found their way to brand-new careers. The phrase "working identity," of course, carries two meanings. It is, first, our sense of self in our professional roles, what we convey about ourselves to others and, ultimately, how we live our working lives. But it can also denote action—a process of applying effort to reshape that identity. Working our identity, I found, is a matter of skill, not personality, and therefore can be learned by almost anyone seeking professional renewal. But first we have to be willing to abandon everything we have ever been taught about making sound career decisions.

A Three-Point Plan

We like to think that the key to a successful career change is knowing what we want to do next, then using that knowledge to guide our actions. But studying people in the throes of the career change process (as opposed to afterward, when hindsight is always 20/20) led me to a startling conclusion: Change actually happens the other way around. Doing comes first, knowing second.

Why? Because changing careers means redefining our working identity. Career change follows a first-act-and-then-think sequence because who we are and what we do are tightly connected, the result of years of action; to change that connection, we must also resort to action—exactly what the conventional wisdom cautions us against.

Conventional career change methods—Susan's "logical" CV progression, Harris's networking, and Gary's planning—are all part of what I call the "plan and implement" model of change. It goes like this: First, determine with as much clarity and certainty as possible what you really want to do. Next, use that knowledge to identify jobs or fields in which your passions can be coupled with your skills and experience. Seek advice from the people who know you best and from professionals in tune with the market. Then simply implement the resulting action steps. Change is seen as a one-shot deal: The plan-and-implement approach cautions us against making a move before we know exactly where we are going.

It all sounds reasonable, and it is a reassuring way to proceed. Yet my research suggests that proceeding this way will lead to the most disastrous of results, which is to say no result. So if your deepest desire is to remain indefinitely in a career that grates on your nerves or stifles your self-expression, simply adhere to that conventional wisdom, presented below as a foolproof, three-point plan.

Know Thyself

Like Gary McCarthy, most of us are taught to begin a career change with a quest for self-knowledge. Knowing, in theory, comes from self-reflection, in solitary introspection or with the help of standardized questionnaires and certified professionals. Learning whether we are introverted or extroverted, whether we prefer to work in a structured and methodical environment or in chaos, whether we place greater value on impact or income helps us avoid jobs that will again prove unsatisfying. Having reached an understanding of his or her temperament, needs, competencies, core values, and priorities, a person can go out and find a job or organization that matches.

Gary did all these things. Armed with his test results, he researched promising companies and industries and networked with a lot of people to get leads and referrals. He made two lists of possibilities: "conformist" and "nonconformist." But what happened from there, and what consumed 90% of the year he spent looking for a new career, is what the conventional models leave out—a lot of trial and error.

Gary started with several rounds of talking with traditional companies and headhunters. Next, he tried to turn a passion or a hobby into a career: He and his wife wrote a business plan for a wine-tour business. The financials were not great, so they dropped it. Next, he pursued his true fantasy career: Gary got certified as a scuba instructor and looked into the purchase of a dive operation. He soon learned, though, that his dream job was unlikely to hold his interest over the long term (and thus was not worth the economic sacrifice). So he went back to the headhunters and traditional companies, only to reconfirm that he did not want what they had to offer. Next, he identified entrepreneurs he admired and looked for ways to get his foot in their doors. He explored freelancing, trying to get short-term projects in exciting young companies. But a precise match did not materialize.

Certainly the common practice of looking back over our careers and identifying what we liked and disliked, what we found satisfying and not satisfying, can be a useful tool. But too often this practice is rooted in the profound misconception that it is possible to discover one's "true self," when the reality is that none of us has such an essence. (See the sidebar "Our Many Possible Selves" for a discussion of why one's true self is so elusive.) Intense introspection also poses the danger that a potential career changer will get stuck in the realm of daydreams. Either the fantasy never finds a match in a real-world, paycheck-producing job or, unlike Gary, we remain emotionally attached to a fantasy career that we do not realize we have outgrown.

We learn who we have become—in practice, not in theory—by testing fantasy and reality, not by "looking inside." Knowing oneself is crucial, but it is usually the outcome of—and not a first input to—the reinvention process. Worse, starting out by trying to identify one's true self often causes paralysis. While we wait for the flash of blinding insight, opportunities pass us by. To launch ourselves anew, we need to get out of our heads. We need to *act*.

Consult Trusted Advisers

If you accept the conventional wisdom that career change begins with self-knowledge and proceeds through an objective scrutiny of the available choices, who should you turn to for guidance? Conventional wisdom has it that you should look to those who know you best and those who know the market. Friends and family—with whom you share a long history—can

Our Many Possible Selves

WHAT IS IDENTITY? Most traditional definitions—the ones that form the foundation for most career advice—are based on the notion of an "inner core" or a "true self." By early adulthood, these theories suggest, a person has formed a relatively stable personality structure, defined by his or her aptitudes, preferences, and values. Excavating this true self—often forgotten in a dead-end pursuit of fame, fortune, or social approval—should be the starting point of any career reorientation, according to conventional wisdom. With the appropriate self-knowledge, obtained via introspection and psychological testing, a person can more easily search for the right "match" and avoid the mistakes of the past. This true-self definition corresponds perfectly to the plan-and-implement method—once we find the self, all that remains is execution.

The work of Stanford cognitive psychologist Hazel Markus and other behavioral scientists, however, offers a different definition of identity, one that is more consistent with what I have discovered: We are many selves. And while these selves are defined partly by our histories, they are defined just as powerfully by our present circumstances and our hopes and fears for the future.

Our possible selves—the images and fantasies we all have about who we hope to become, think we should become, or even fear becoming—are at the heart of the career change process. Although conventional wisdom says pain—a self we fear becoming—is the only driver for change, in reality pain can create paralysis. We change only when we have enticing alternatives that we can feel, touch, and taste. That is why working identity, as a practice,

offer insight into your true nature, and they have your best interests at heart; professionals add a dose of pragmatism, keeping you grounded in the realities of the marketplace.

In times of change and uncertainty, we naturally take comfort in our enduring connections with friends and is necessarily a process of experimenting, testing, and learning about our possible selves.

Take Gary McCarthy, the former investment banker and consultant profiled in the main article. The set of possible selves he considered is typical in its number and range. It included a "ditch it all and open a tour-guide business in the south of France with my wife" self; a socially respectable "junior partner" self that his parents would have endorsed; a youthful, outdoorsy, "follow your passion" self who renounced convention and wanted to open a scuba business; a "responsible spouse and future parent" self who wanted to make good dual-career decisions; a "corporate drone at age 50, full of regrets" self; an "apprentice" self who learned at the elbow of an admired entrepreneur; and a practical, reasonable, "go to a traditional company where I can combine my backgrounds in banking and consulting" self.

Conventional wisdom would say that the scope of his list of possibilities was evidence that he lacked focus and wasn't ready for change. But within the working identity framework, it was precisely this variety that allowed him to find a truly good fit. Certain possible selves are concrete and tangible, defined by the things we do and the company we keep today; others remain vague and fuzzy, existing only in the realm of private dreams, hypothetical possibilities, and abstract ideas. By bringing the possibilities—both desired and feared, present and future—more sharply into focus, we give ourselves a concrete base of experience from which to choose among them.

family. But when it comes to reinventing ourselves, the people who know us best are the ones most likely to hinder rather than help us. They may wish to be supportive, but they tend to reinforce—or even desperately try to preserve—the old identities we are trying to shed. Early in his career, Gary discovered that his close circle would not be much help. "I wanted to do something different but was shocked to realize that people were already pigeonholing me," he says. "I tried to brainstorm with friends and family about what other things I might do. All the ideas that came back were a version of 'Well, you could get a middle management job in a finance department of a company.' Or 'You could become a trainee in a management program.'" John Alexander, an investment banker hoping to make a go of fiction writing, reports that he had often discussed his career predicament with his friends and family. "They would tend to say, 'I can see why writing might be interesting, but you've got a very good job, and do you really want to jeopardize that?'"

Mentors and close coworkers, though well meaning, can also unwittingly hold us back. Take Harris Roberts, the health care company director who wanted to assume a general management role. The people around him, who were invested in his staying put, only mirrored his normal doubts about moving outside his comfort zone. His mentors cared about him and held the power to make his desired change a reality. But they made a fence, not a gateway, blocking the moves that would lead to career change. By talking only to people who inhabited his immediate professional world, people whose ideas for him didn't go beyond the four walls, Harris seriously limited himself. Not only did he lack outside market information, but these coworkers could no more let go of their outdated image of a junior Harris than he himself could.

Headhunters and outplacers, today's career change professionals, can keep us tethered to the past just as effectively. We assume, rightly, that they have the market perspective we lack—but we forget that they are in the business of facilitating incremental moves along an established trajectory. At midcareer, however, many people are no longer looking to "leverage past experience in a different setting." They want to invent their own jobs and escape the shackles of corporate convention, in some cases to do something completely different. What Susan Fontaine, the management consultant, experienced is typical: "I found headhunters unhelpful, basically. I would say, 'Here are my skills; what else might I do?' And they kept saying, 'Why don't you move to Andersen?' or, 'Why don't you try Bain?' All they could suggest was exactly the same thing. I kept saying, 'I'm quite clear I don't want to do that, and if I did want to do that, I would not come to you. I can do that on my own.'"

So if self-assessment, the advice of close ones, and the counsel of change professionals won't do it, then where can we find support for our reinvention? To make a true break with the past, we need to see ourselves in a new light. We need guides who have been there and can understand where we are going. Reaching outside our normal circles to new people, networks, and professional communities is the best way to both break frame and get psychological sustenance.

Think Big

We like to think that we can leap directly from a desire for change to a single decision that will complete our reinvention—the conventional wisdom would say you shouldn't fool yourself with small, superficial adjustments. But trying to tackle the big changes too quickly can be counterproductive. Just as starting the transition by looking for one's true self can cause paralysis rather than progress, trying to make one big move once and for all can prevent real change.

When Susan Fontaine decided to leave her consulting career, it was with good reason. A single mother of two, she was finding the travel and other demands on her personal life increasingly intolerable. She quit her job and resolved to spend some time exploring her options. That resolve vanished, however, when financial pressure coincided with a flattering offer to join the management team of a former client. She accepted the new position only to discover that its demands would be very similar to those of the position she had left. "I thought, 'What have I done?'" she later told me. "I had had the opportunity to leave all that!" By hoping to solve all her problems in one fell swoop, Susan made a change that amounted to no change at all. Two weeks into the new job, she resigned.

As much as we might want to avoid endless procrastination, premature closure is not the answer. It takes time to discover what we truly want to change and to identify the deeply grooved habits and assumptions that are holding us back. The lesson of Susan's story is that trying to make a single bold move can bring us back to square one all too quickly. A longer, less linear transition process may leave us feeling that we are wasting time. But as we will see below, taking smaller steps can allow a richer, more grounded redefinition of our working identity to emerge.

Three Success Stories

Although they floundered, victims of conventional wisdom, Gary McCarthy, Harris Roberts, and Susan Fontaine eventually moved on to a different—and more successful—approach. Gary is now at a media company he admires, working as an internal venture capitalist, a role that allows him to use his skill set in consulting and finance but grants him great creative latitude and total ownership of his results. Harris is president and COO of a growing medical device company and very much involved in setting the strategic direction of his new firm. Susan is working with non-profits, bringing her strategy expertise to this sector and loving her work.

None of them followed a straight and narrow route. Gary dabbled in wine tours and flirted with buying a scuba diving operation before settling on what his wife called a more normal path. Harris had his prized general management role snatched from under him a second time as the result of a corporate restructuring. He considered leaving for a biotech start-up but realized that he simply did not have the appetite for such a risky move. Susan set up temporarily as a freelance consultant, landing traditional consulting projects to pay the bills and using her discretionary time to explore a more varied portfolio of assignments.

Their experience is typical. Nearly everyone who tries to figure out a next career takes a long time to find the one that is truly right. Most career transitions take about three years. It is rarely a linear path: We take two steps forward and one step back, and where we end up often surprises us.

Working Identity

Once we start questioning not just whether we are in the right job or organization today but also what we thought we wanted for the future, the job search methods we have all been taught fail us. But that doesn't mean we must resign ourselves to a random process governed by factors outside our control—life crisis that forces us to reprioritize, an unexpected job offer. There is an alternative method that works according to a different logic than the plan-and-implement approach. Gary, Harris, and Susan, as well as many other successful career changers I have observed, shared this method, which I call the "test and learn" model of change. During times of transition—when our possible selves are shifting wildly—the only way to create change is by putting our possible identities into practice, working and crafting them until they are sufficiently grounded in experience to guide more decisive steps. (See the sidebar "Test and Learn.")

The test-and-learn approach recognizes that the only way to counter uncertainty and resist the pull of the familiar is to make alternative futures more vivid, more tangible, and more doable. We acquired our old identities in practice. Likewise, we redefine them, in prac-

Test and Learn

YOUR WORKING IDENTITY is an amalgam of the kind of work you do, the relationships and organizations that form part of your work life, and the story you tell about why you do what you do and how you arrived at that point. Reshaping that identity, therefore, is a matter of making adjustments to all three of those aspects over time. The adjustments happen tentatively and incrementally, so the process can seem disorderly. In fact, it is a logical process of testing, discovering, and adapting that can be learned by almost anyone seeking professional renewal.

Crafting experiments

Working identity is defined by what we do, the professional activities that engage us. ▶	Try out new activities and professional roles on a small scale before making a major commitment to a different path.

Shifting connections

Working identity is also defined by the company we keep, our working relationships, and the ▶ professional groups to which we belong.	Develop contacts that can open doors to new worlds, and look for role models and new reference groups to guide and benchmark your progress.

Making sense

Working identity is also defined by the formative events in our lives and the stories that link ▶ who we were and who we will become.	Find or create catalysts and triggers for change, and use them as occasions to rework your life story.

tice, by crafting experiments, shifting connections, and making sense of the changes we are going through. These three common practices lie at the heart of the most disparate of career changes, lending logic to what can look like chance occurrences and disorderly behavior.

Crafting Experiments

By far the biggest mistake people make when trying to change careers is delaying the first step until they have settled on a destination. This error is undermining because the only way we figure out what we really want to do is by giving it a try. Understandably, most people are reluctant to leap into the unknown. We must test our fantasies—otherwise, they remain just that. I discovered that most people create new working identities on the side at first, by getting involved in extracurricular ventures and weekend projects.

Crafting experiments refers to the practice of creating these side projects. Their great advantage is that we can try out new professional roles on a limited scale without compromising our current jobs or having to leap into new positions too quickly. In almost every instance of successful change that I have observed, the person had already been deeply engaged in the new career for quite some time.

There are many ways to set up experiments that work. Newly resolved to explore a range of possibilities, Susan took freelancing assignments in her old line of work and did pro bono work for charities as her lifeline to get her through this difficult period. Through that work, she began to develop contacts that led to paid charity consulting. Gradually, she became immersed in nonprofits, a sector she had never expected to find a career in. And she found herself enjoying freelancing. Today, she is working with the largest UK consulting firm that specializes in charities, and she has this to say: "All I hope is that I never again make the mistake of jumping before giving myself the chance to explore what I really want to do."

Other people use temporary assignments, outside contracts, advisory work, and moonlighting to get experience or build skills in new industries. Thanks to a temporary stint at the helm of his division, Harris got over his fear, which had silently plagued him for years, that he lacked the finance and cross-functional background necessary to be a good general manager. This concrete experience, more than any amount of self-reflection, helped him envision himself as a general manager. Taking courses or picking up training and credentials in a new area is still another way of experimenting. For many of the people in my study, an executive program, sabbatical, or extended vacation improved their capacity to move in a new direction. These breaks are powerful because they force us to step back from the daily routine while engaging us with new people and activities.

Shifting Connections

Consider how common it is for employees to say of their companies, "There is no one here I want to be like." At midcareer, our desire for change is rarely about only the work we do; it is perhaps more importantly about changing our working relationships so they are more satisfying and inspiring. Shifting connections refers to the practice of finding people who can help us see and grow into our new selves. For most successful career changers I have observed, a guiding figure or new professional community helped to light the way and cushion the eventual leap.

Finding a new job always requires networking outside our usual circles. We get ideas and job leads by
branching out. Gary, for example, used his alumni and
company networks quite successfully. It was an ex-
employee of his company—someone he didn't know
personally—who got him the temporary project at his
current company. But what clinched his decision, what
made this job different from all the other conformist
roles he had considered, was the opportunity to work
for a role model he had long admired and from whom
he could learn the ropes.

Seeking refuge in close working relationships is natural in times of change and uncertainty. But Harris made
a classic mistake in turning to an old mentor, Alfred,
who was too invested in Harris remaining the unsure
protégé to give him room to grow. Harris's way out of
this "codependent" relationship came via a person he
had met casually at a professional conference. Gerry,
the company founder who later hired Harris as his COO,
initially approached Harris for regulatory advice. Eventually, they developed an informal consulting relationship. In Gerry, Harris found a person who believed in his
potential as a general manager and offered a different
kind of close, interdependent working relationship: "It
was such a contrast to my relationship with Alfred,"
Harris says. "It's not as paternal. Gerry knows things
I need to learn—things that re late to creative financing,
ways to raise money—but he also needs to learn from
me. He doesn't know how to run a company, and I do.
He's looking to me to teach him what's necessary to
develop an organization, to build a foundation. I think

I can learn a lot from Gerry, but it's a more mature and more professional relationship than I had with Alfred."

To make a break with the past, we must venture into unknown networks—and not just for job leads. Often it is strangers who are best equipped to help us see who we are becoming.

Making Sense

In the middle of the confusion about which way to go, many of us hope for one event that will clarify everything, that will transform our stumbling moves into a coherent trajectory. Julio Gonzales, a doctor trying to leave the practice of medicine, put it like this: "I was waiting for an epiphany—I wake up in the middle of the night and the Angel of Mercy tells me *this* is what I should do." The third working identity practice, making sense, refers to creating our own triggers for change: infusing events—the momentous and the mundane—with special meaning and weaving them into a story about who we are becoming.

Every person who has changed careers has a story about the moment of truth. For John Alexander, the would-be author I've mentioned, the moment of truth came when, on a whim, he visited an astrologer. To his surprise, the first thing she said to him was, "I'm glad I haven't been *you* for the last two or three years. You have been undergoing a painful internal tug-of-war between two opposing factions. One side wants stability, economic well-being, and social status, and the other craves artistic expression, maybe as a writer or an impresario. You may wish to believe that there can be reconciliation between these two. I tell you, there cannot be." Another career changer, a woman who had grown increasingly frustrated as an executive in a high-tech start-up, said, "One day my husband just asked me, 'Are you happy? If you are, that's great. But you don't *look* happy.' His question prompted me to reconsider what I was doing."

It would be easy to believe from such accounts that career changes have their geneses in such moments. But the moment of insight is an effect, not a cause, of change. Across my many interviews, a striking discovery was that such moments tended to occur late in the transition process, only after much trial and tribulation. Rather than catalyzing change, defining moments helped people make sense of changes that had long been unfolding.

Trigger events don't just jolt us out of our habitual routines, they are the necessary pegs on which to hang our reinvention stories. Arranging life events into a coherent story is one of the subtlest, yet most demanding, challenges of career reinvention. To reinvent oneself is to rework one's story. At the start of a career transition, when all we have is a laundry list of diffuse ideas, it unsettles us that we have no story. It disturbs us to find so many different options appealing, and we worry that the same self who once chose what we no longer want to do might again make a bad choice. Without a story that explains why we must change, the external audience to whom we are selling our reinvention remains dubious, and we, too, feel unsettled and uncertain.

Good stories develop in the telling and retelling, by being put into the public sphere even before they are fully formed. Instead of being embarrassed about having visited an astrologer, for example, John told everyone his story and even wrote about it in a newspaper column. The closer he got to finding his creative outlet, the more the episode made sense and the less often his story elicited the "Why would you want to do that?" reaction. By making public declarations about what we seek and about the common thread that binds our old and new selves, we clarify our intentions and improve our ability to enlist others' support.

The Road Now Taken

Most of us know what we are trying to escape: the lockstep of a narrowly defined career, inauthentic or unstimulating work, numbing corporate politics, a lack of time for life outside of work. Finding an alternative that truly fits, like finding one's mission in life, cannot be accomplished overnight. It takes time, perseverance, and hard work. But effort isn't enough; a sound method and the skill to put it into practice are also required.

The idea of working one's identity flies in the face of everything we have always been told about choosing careers. It asks us to devote the greater part of our time and energy to action rather than reflection, to doing instead of planning. It tells us to give up the search for a ten-point plan and to accept instead a crooked path. But what appears to be a mysterious, road-to-Damascus process is actually a learning-by-doing practice that any of us can adopt. We start by taking action.

HERMINIA IBARRA is a professor of organizational behavior at Insead in France and the author of *Working Identity: Unconventional Strategies for Reinventing Your Career* (Harvard Business Review Press, 2003).

Originally published in December 2002. Reprint RO212B

Job-Hopping to the Top and Other Career Fallacies

by Monika Hamori

CLIMBING THE HIERARCHY USED to be a reward for loyalty. But in the 1980s, as firms stripped out layers of management, promotions became fewer and farther between. To get ahead, executives started moving from company to company. A 2009 survey by career network ExecuNet found that executives now stay with an organization for only 3.3 years, on average, before moving on. Outside job changes outnumber internal ones by about two to one.

But is it true that switching employers offers a fast track to the top jobs? According to my research, the answer is no. In fact, that's one of four career fallacies I identified in a study examining how managers get ahead. Understanding the reality behind job moves gives executives a leg up when planning for the future.

Fallacy 1: Job-Hoppers Prosper

The notion that you get ahead faster by switching companies is reinforced by career counselors, who advise people to keep a constant eye on outside opportunities. But the data show that footloose executives are not more upwardly mobile than their single-company colleagues.

My analysis of the career histories of 1,001 chief executive officers who lead the largest corporations in Europe and the U.S. reveals that CEOs have worked, on average, for just three employers during their careers. And although lifetime employment is increasingly rare, a quarter of the CEOs I looked at spent an entire career with the same firm. Overall, the more years people stayed with a company, the faster they made it to the top.

CEOs are arguably a special population, so I also analyzed the job changes of 14,000 non-CEO executives to compare the outcomes of their inside and outside moves. Again, inside moves produced a considerably higher percentage and faster pace of promotions.

One likely reason that internal candidates do better is that companies know more about them; promoting an insider poses less risk than hiring somebody from the outside, no matter how extensive the CV or how detailed the reference. Executive search firms show a preference for stability as well—which is ironic, given that they're the ones in the business of shuttling professionals from job to job. One U.S. boutique firm specializing in IT evaluates candidates on two axes:

Idea in Brief

Executives stay with an organization for only 3.3 years, on average. But does switching employers offer a fast-track to the top jobs? Research suggests the answer is no. In fact, that's one of four career fallacies identified in a study examining how managers get ahead. Fallacy 1: Job hoppers prosper. An analysis of the career histories of 1,001 CEOs and 14,000 non-CEOs in top corporations shows that the more years executives stay with the company, the faster they make it to the top.
Lesson: Build a résumé that demonstrates a balance between external and internal moves. Fallacy 2: A move should be a move up. Among the executives studied, about 40% of job changes were promotions, 40% were lateral, and 25% were demotions.
Lesson: While a downward move will detract from your CV, a lateral move can often lead to a promotion or enhance

your CV when the new company conveys brand value.
Fallacy 3: Big fish swim in big ponds. When making a move, 64% of executives trade down to smaller, less-recognized firms. They gain better titles or positions, cashing in on the brand value of their former employer. Lesson: Join top companies as early in your career as you can, and transfer to a lesser company only if the job is very attractive.
Fallacy 4: Career and industry switchers are penalized. It's not always a bad move to change industries, or even careers, as is often assumed. Firms hire employees from different businesses for many reasons: For example, another industry might simply offer superior human capital.
Lesson: Look for industries where your skills represent a genuine asset. Every career is unique; what's important is to look at each move with a critical eye.

stability and "performance and capability indicators." Candidates have to score well on both to be selected for interviews. A consultant at another firm told me that a short stint—less than three years or so—probably wouldn't be sufficient to produce any meaningful contribution to a firm and thus wouldn't do much to demonstrate a candidate's value. Search consultants also tend to interpret frequent moves as a sign of bad decision making, whereas long organizational tenure is rarely seen as reaching a plateau.

There are exceptions, of course. In smaller industries, for instance, where "everybody knows everybody," companies that recruit from competitors can be stigmatized as poachers. And frequent moves are unacceptable in certain countries. A midcareer Spanish manager who has worked in Japan for almost 10 years told me that leaving a job is culturally seen as treachery. Expat professionals are particularly limited in their movements because their working visas are sponsored by their employers.

Lessons for Executives

First, know that search firms are looking for résumés that demonstrate a balance between external and internal moves. One finance-search-firm recruiter I interviewed put it this way: "We like people with two or three companies. And then you look at the patterns: ideally, 10 years in one employer, two or three years in the next, but then we want to see another eight-year run." Many search firms are looking for evidence that an executive is integrating with and being rewarded by the people who work with him or her.

Second, remember that a significant proportion of executives succeed by sticking it out with one company, so consider cross-employer moves only if they'll considerably increase your employability.

Fallacy 2: A Move Should Be a Move Up

A job change, whether internal or external, doesn't necessarily mean a promotion, despite the perception that careers generally follow an upward trajectory. In reality, many changes are lateral moves, even among relatively successful executives.

In my research, the moves that constituted promotions met at least one of two criteria: They resulted in a better title with more responsibility or propelled the executive to a larger firm. Such job changes represented about 40% of the data set. Lateral moves—across division, geography, or industry—were equally common. And 20% of the job changes reflected downward moves—a lesser title or narrower scope of responsibility or a lateral move to a much smaller organization. (Smaller size implies less managerial complexity.) I found that large promotions (that is, considerable jumps in both title and employer size) were relatively uncommon—less than 5%.

While step-downs generally detract from a CV, a lateral move is by no means a career killer. It may in fact prove beneficial in the long run if done wisely. For instance, a lateral move may be justified by the prospect of a promotion in the near future.

One employee I'll call Robert, for example, recently made a lateral move, from a managerial position at one industrial maintenance company to a consultative role at another. (All names have been changed for purposes of privacy.) But the new job offers the potential for entry into the executive ranks. His new boss is the VP for strategy, and Robert works with high-potential employees on projects that involve the COO and the CEO. He is now tied to the most important work and has become visible to top management. After 18 months, the company intends to reassign the high potentials, and Robert is in line for an executive post.

Lateral moves often enhance CVs when the new company conveys brand value. Robert's new firm has networks in many growing or high-profile industries like environmental protection and oil and gas—giving Robert a valuable set of contacts and a variety of learning opportunities. A lateral move into a different industry can broaden and deepen expertise, as well.

Lessons for Executives

Fast upward leaps may not secure long-term success; often, a slower ascent that includes a mixture of lateral and upward movement is what pays off. One multinational food company with more than 60,000 employees constructs a personalized, 10-year development plan for each high potential. A strong generalist view of the business (including knowledge of finance, marketing, and how to manage people) is the determining factor in making it to the top executive ranks. Many companies share this belief, valuing employees who switch between functional tracks and general management.

To be sure, those who remain in a single function may move faster in the first part of their career, but they soon reach a ceiling because they're too specialized. One of the top executives at the food company has been an employee for almost 20 years, having held one- to three-year stints in nine countries, worked in three functional areas, and switched several times between managerial and consultative roles. Although his moves always bumped him up in the company's job grade system, not all may have seemed like advancements on paper.

Also bear in mind that a move that's technically a promotion may turn out to be a detour. Another executive, Michael, worked in the corporate legal office of a multinational tech company with more 20,000 employees; when he was offered the chance to become the head of the legal department in one of the firm's seven business units, he jumped at the opportunity. He got a title change and new managerial responsibilities, and he reported directly to the business unit CEO. But it turned out to be a dead-end job, because Michael didn't work well with the chief executive. His compensation took a severe hit: Although his base salary stayed the same, he suffered a substantial cut both in his bonus and in his stock option plans.

It's easy to be distracted by a better title, a bigger pool of direct reports, or other trappings, so when making a switch, always consider what the next move might be and to what extent the current move will help or hinder your ability to achieve longer-term goals.

Fallacy 3: Big Fish Swim in Big Ponds

Big-name companies like Goldman Sachs and Morgan Stanley often appear to "swap" professionals. They have similar cultures, so people believe they recruit from their peers in order to get high-quality employees. They're also looking for valuable insider expertise.

But the data show that when executives leave well-known companies, they more typically trade down to smaller, less-recognized firms. In my data set, 64% of executives who left an admired company—as measured by its presence on *Fortune*'s Most Admired or a similar list—transferred to a firm not included on the list. (Of course, one reason people trade down is that there are fewer and fewer positions available at big-name companies as they climb the ranks.)

Those who leave for lesser-known or less highly regarded companies often gain in terms of title or position. In other words, they cash in on the brand value of their former employer. On the flip side, those who transfer to organizations with stronger reputations seem more willing to take a step down in position—to pay a price to acquire some brand value.

Lessons for Executives

Obviously you should do your best to join well-regarded companies as early in your career as you can. Future employers and search firms tend to equate corporate brand names with knowledge and skills. Said one consultant at a large multinational, "You can tell what competencies senior executives have just by looking at which organization they belonged to." A headhunter at a smaller, boutique firm told me: "If you know that a person is with that company, you have already made a step in the right direction in terms of qualifying them."

The Real Story

AS THE DATA SHOW, some career moves make more sense than others and the conventional wisdom doesn't necessarily hold true.

Fallacy 1: Job-Hoppers Prosper

30% of moves from one organization to another are demotions

10% of inside moves are demotions

Fallacy 2: A Move Should Be a Move Up

4% of job changes are large promotions

34% are modest promotions

Fallacy 3: Big Fish Swim in Big Ponds

8% of moves from a big name to a small name involve a step down in title

24% of moves from a small name to a big name involve a step down

Fallacy 4: Industry Switchers Are Penalized

10% started career with no industry experience

49% of CEOs at the largest firms in Europe and Asia had experience in more than one industry

17% had experience in three or more industries

You should transfer to a lesser company only if the career opportunity is very attractive, beyond a jump in title and salary; otherwise it can limit your prospects down the road. Back to Michael, described earlier—he joined a big law firm after passing the bar but left to follow his boss to a niche firm that specialized in legal advice to the maritime business. He received a 50% pay increase with the move.

Soon, however, he regretted his decision, and after only two years he wanted to move again. This time he

About the Research

THESE FINDINGS ON CAREER fallacies come from my eight-year research project using four sources of data:

1. 14,000 career histories of executives in four sectors of the financial services industry, drawn from the records of one of the largest multinational executive-search firms;

2. the career histories of the CEOs of the 2005 *Financial Times* Europe 500 and the U.S. Standard & Poor's 500 (a total of 1,001 CEOs because one firm has co-CEOs). The CEOs are located in the United States and in 21 European countries;

3. semistructured interviews with 45 executive search consultants at both large, multinational search firms and specialized boutiques (all U.S.-based);

4. interviews and online discussions with more than 20 alumni of IE Business School's executive MBA program. Interviewees were typically mid-career professionals (late thirties, early forties) living in Europe, Asia, or North or South America. Their work experience ranged from 10 to 20 years.

had trouble finding a suitable job and realized that his stint at the niche firm had damaged his prospects. Michael said that potential employers "looked down on" him and saw him as unable to fit in at a large firm. He knew that the training and professional development he had received in the large firm from his boss had continued in the new position. But that didn't matter to recruiters—it was the firm name that counted. He eventually found a job in the public sector, but to this day he feels that his move limited his options.

Fallacy 4: Career and Industry Switchers Are Penalized

While you'd think that changing industries or careers (a function change, for instance) would set you back, switchers don't fare worse in terms of promotions than those who stick to one field or specialize. Changing to a new area is relatively common—29% of moves take people across industries and another 23% across different segments of the same industry (going from a consumer finance company to a bank, for example).

Why would a firm hire employees from a different business? In some cases, another industry might simply offer superior human capital. One consultant at a search firm specializing in the hotel, gaming, and restaurant industries told me that 40% of his work involved recruiting from outside that world. "I am looking for companies that continuously produce high quality. If the client wants somebody who has classic marketing skills, I go to Procter & Gamble. For a very aggressive P&L background, I may go to PepsiCo."

Another executive search consultant, this one in financial services, had a similar experience: The paucity of talent in the private equity arena made hiring overly expensive. Most industry candidates came from just two major investment banks, and those executives commanded outrageous compensation. By looking at adjacent industries—pension funds, for instance, or asset management—he could produce candidates who had, as he put it, "the right wiring and intellectual capability to learn the private equity product," at a cheaper price. He could hire an executive from a global asset firm for about $800,000 to $1 million. The same person coming from the private equity space would have cost two or three times as much, maybe more.

Even candidates who lack industry experience may match the hiring company's needs at other levels. An executive we'll call Steven made the switch from textiles to chemicals because he had a strong track record in sales and his new company had a sales-driven culture.

When hiring companies are not sufficiently attractive to job seekers, they often need to expand their searches. In one instance, the majority owner of another sales-driven company required that all professionals—even those entering at a managerial or executive level—spend some four to six months in the sales organization. That was unappealing to many applicants; half the candidates dropped out right after their interviews because the job didn't seem to match what they saw as their strengths. So to find the best people, the company had to broaden its searches.

Lessons for Executives
Look strategically for industries where your skills represent a genuine asset. Some specializations are very difficult to find and thus worth a premium to those seeking them. A former navy pilot, Marcus, got a job as a financial analyst with SunTrust at a 50% salary increase despite having no industry expertise, because the company was looking for knowledge of the defense sector. Three years later, he headed the department.

Consider, also, a transitional job. One manager I met recently moved from a law firm, where he was marketing director, to a consultancy specializing in relocation, expatriation, and cross-cultural training. His goal was to become a consultant—a change in both industry and function—but he knew it would be almost impossible to do both at once. So he accepted the marketing-manager position at the consulting firm. He even took a pay cut, but the job allows him to learn about cross-cultural management and, he hopes, ultimately achieve his career goals.

Every career is unique, and a move that's right for you might turn out to be disastrous for your colleague, even one whose résumé and career goals are similar to yours. The fallacies I've identified are based on the experiences of real executives making real choices—but it could be that, for instance, job-hopping is the quickest way to the top in your case. What's important is to look at each move with a critical eye, putting aside conventional wisdom and other people's assumptions to make the choice that fits your own ambitions.

MONIKA HAMORI is a professor of human resource management at IE Business School in Madrid.

Originally published in July 2010. Reprint R1007Q

Are You a High Potential?

by Douglas A. Ready, Jay A. Conger, and Linda A. Hill

SOME EMPLOYEES ARE MORE talented than others. That's a fact of organizational life that few executives and HR managers would dispute. The more debatable point is how to treat the people who appear to have the highest potential. Opponents of special treatment argue that all employees are talented in some way and, therefore, all should receive equal opportunities for growth. Devoting a disproportionate amount of energy and resources to a select few, their thinking goes, might cause you to overlook the potential contributions of the many. But the disagreement doesn't stop there. Some executives say that a company's list of high potentials—and the process for creating it—should be a closely guarded secret. After all, why dampen motivation among the roughly 95% of employees who aren't on the list?

For the past 15 to 20 years, we've been studying programs for high-potential leaders. Most recently we surveyed 45 companies worldwide about how they identify and develop these people. We then interviewed HR executives at a dozen of those companies to gain insights about the experiences they provide for high potentials and about the criteria for getting and staying on the list. Then, guided by input from HR leaders, we met with and interviewed managers they'd designated as rising stars.

Our research makes clear that high-potential talent lists exist, whether or not companies acknowledge them and whether the process for developing them is formal or informal. Of the companies we studied, 98% reported that they purposefully identify high potentials. Especially when resources are constrained, companies *do* place disproportionate attention on developing the people they think will lead their organizations into the future.

So you might be asking yourself, "How do I get—and stay—on my company's high-potential list?" This article can help you begin to answer that question. Think of it as a letter to the millions of smart, competent, hardworking, trustworthy employees who are progressing through their careers with some degree of satisfaction but are still wondering how to get where they really want to go. We'll look at the specific qualities of managers whose firms identified them as having made the grade.

The Anatomy of a High Potential

Let's begin with our definition of a high-potential employee. Your company may have a different definition

Idea in Brief

Some employees are more talented than others, and nearly every company has its method for identifying their high-potential managers. So how can you get on your company's high-potential list? Douglas A. Ready, of the talent-management research center ICEDR; Jay A. Conger, of Claremont McKenna College; and Harvard Business School's Linda A. Hill have studied programs for high-potential leaders for 15 years. They have found that the rising stars who make the grade are remarkably similar in their core characteristics, the most intangible of which they call "X factors": a drive to excel, a catalytic learning capability, an enterprising spirit, and dynamic sensors that detect opportunities and obstacles. The authors' in-depth interviews with high potentials, their managers, and their HR departments reveal how you can develop your four X factors and, if you manage to get on your company's high-potential list, how to avoid falling off. The article also discusses the pros and cons companies face as they decide whether to make their high-potential lists transparent.

or might not even officially distinguish high potentials from other employees. However, our research has shown that companies tend to think of the top 3% to 5% of their talent in these terms:

High potentials consistently and significantly outperform their peer groups in a variety of settings and circumstances. While achieving these superior levels of performance, they exhibit behaviors that reflect their companies' culture and values in an exemplary manner. Moreover, they show a strong capacity to grow and succeed throughout their careers within an organization—more quickly and effectively than their peer groups do.

That's the basic anatomy of a high potential. Gaining membership in this elite group starts with three essential elements.

Deliver Strong Results—Credibly

Making your numbers is important, but it isn't enough. You'll never get on a high-potential list if you don't perform with distinction or if your results come at the expense of someone else. Competence is the baseline quality for high performance. But you also need to prove your credibility. That means building trust and confidence among your colleagues and, thereby, influencing a wide array of stakeholders.

Look at Jackie Goodwin, a bank executive cited by her HR department as a high potential. Jackie started out in the insurance division but wanted to switch to banking, which she perceived as a career path with more room for growth. Her general management skills were highly regarded, and she had a proven track record in financial services within insurance. The banking side's desire for new blood and a lack of succession planning in the region positioned her well as an outsider. Indeed, her record was as strong—if not stronger—than that of the insiders.

When Jackie was offered a stretch assignment in the banking division—a promotion to vice president and regional operating officer in Germany, the bank's second largest European operation—she accepted it, even though the odds were against her. Nobody there had heard of her, and she knew little about banking. What's more, she'd been forced on the regional president, who wanted someone with experience. Her biggest challenge was to gain credibility. The German staff was accustomed to running its own show, so Jackie figured she'd fail if she couldn't get the team on her side.

Jackie resolved to make helping her new colleagues a priority. In her first three weeks, she met with dozens of managers and openly acknowledged that she faced a steep learning curve. She also focused on achieving small wins on issues that had long been thorns in their sides. For example, she went out of her way to streamline the process for opening new accounts. As for her skeptical boss, she aimed to take as much off his plate as possible. She would ask, "What time-consuming tasks would you like to see addressed within 90 days?" Then she'd get right to work. For instance, he disliked confrontation, so Jackie tackled issues with potential for conflict, such as redesigning planning processes and resolving decision rights. She gained a reputation as a problem solver, and her influence grew steadily. Today, Jackie is the head of all commercial lending for the bank and is still considered a rising star.

Master New Types of Expertise

Early in your career, getting noticed is all about mastering the technical expertise that the job requires. As you progress, you need to broaden that expertise. You start by managing an employee or a small group, and then move on to larger teams and positions (for instance, at corporate headquarters) that require you to exercise influence despite having limited formal authority. For example, in senior roles technical excellence might fade in value relative to strategic-thinking and motivational skills. At a certain point, you will face the challenge of *letting go* as much as the challenge of *adding on*. Don't aspire, for example, to be the best engineer and the best design team leader at the same time.

For some, such lessons are learned the hard way. One exceptionally talented software engineer, whom we'll call Luke, had won many accolades during a relatively short career. Confident in his potential, Luke's managers put him in charge of a team that was creating a product extension expected to attract a whole new category of users. Luke was well liked and happily took on the challenge, but he failed to recognize that technical skill alone wouldn't suffice. After several missed deadlines, company executives created a face-saving, senior-level "expert" post for him. Meanwhile, they put another technically skilled employee, who also had project-management expertise, in charge. Luke, no longer a high potential, went on to have a fairly distinguished career as a technical expert, but not in an enterprise leadership role.

Recognize That Behavior Counts

Although your performance gets you noticed and promoted early in your career, your behavior is what keeps you on the radar as a high potential. Outstanding skills never really diminish in importance, but they become a given as you are expected to excel in roles with broader reach. Prospective candidates for that coveted high-potential label must demonstrate a behavioral shift from "fit and affiliation" to "role model and teacher."

Should You Tell Her She's a High Potential?

WHETHER OR NOT A COMPANY should make its list of high potentials transparent is an evergreen question. In our surveys of 45 company policies and in our work with firms during the past 15 to 20 years, we have found a growing trend toward transparency. The percentage of companies that inform high potentials of their status has risen from 70% about a decade ago to 85% today. Employers, we believe, are coming to see talent as a strategic resource that, like other types of capital, can move around. Executives are tired of exit interviews in which promising employees say, "If I had known you had plans for me and were serious about following through, I would have stayed."

Nevertheless, making your list of high potentials transparent increases the pressure to do something with the people who are on it. If you tell someone you view her as a future leader, you need to back that up with tangible progress in her professional development. Otherwise, she may feel manipulated and even lose motivation. In one case, we witnessed a near riot at a company offsite, where a group of high potentials said they felt "played"—that their status was just a retention tactic, with no real plans to promote them. Either approach has risks: If you don't make the list public, you might lose your best performers; if you opt for transparency, you'll heighten the expectation of action.

The rise of general manager Phil Nolan to the executive ranks of his company, a market leader in laundry products, was due in large part to his role-model qualities. Phil was placed in charge of the firm's troubled core product, a liquid detergent whose sales were in a multi-year downward slide. Two high-visibility marketing managers had each been given a chance to reinvigorate product sales. Both had tried price-reduction tactics, to no avail. Then it was Phil's turn. But, with a background in product development rather than marketing, he was the dark horse candidate.

Fortunately, corporate executives saw more in Phil, who had engineered a turnaround at a troubled product-development group by fostering cooperative relationships and teamwork. Highly trustworthy, he could engage people in very candid conversations about business challenges. As a result, he was able to get to the core of a problem quickly and find viable solutions. Phil not only was superb at motivating people, but also had a keen eye for patterns and an impressive strategic vision. He applied all those skills to the new assignment.

Within the first year in his new role, Phil led his team to grow product sales by 30%. In our interview with the company's HR executive, she emphasized Phil's ability to win people over: "There is humility to him despite the fact that he is now the public face of the brand. Phil helps his peers succeed rather than threatening them. He is a role model for the organization."

How High Potentials Are Hardwired

You're doing everything right. You're delivering value and early results. You're mastering new areas of expertise as you face increasingly complex challenges. You embrace your organization's culture and values. You exude confidence and have earned the respect of others. Maybe you're regularly putting in a 50-hour week and getting excellent reviews. Nevertheless, high-potential status remains elusive.

This can be infuriating because the real differentiators—what we call the "X factors"—are somewhat intangible and usually don't show up on lists of leadership competencies or on performance review forms. Here are those factors, which can tip the scales and help you achieve and maintain that coveted high-potential rating.

X Factor #1: A Drive to Excel

High potentials aren't just high achievers. They are driven to succeed. Good, even very good, isn't good enough. Not by any stretch. They are more than willing to go that extra mile and realize they may have to make sacrifices in their personal lives in order to advance. That doesn't mean they aren't true to their values, but sheer ambition may lead them to make some pretty hard choices.

X Factor #2: A Catalytic Learning Capability

We often think of high potentials as relentless learners, but a lot of people out there learn continually yet lack an action or results orientation. The high potentials we have come across possess what we call a "catalytic learning capability." They have the capacity to scan for new ideas, the cognitive capability to absorb them, and the common sense to translate that new learning into productive action for their customers and their organizations.

X Factor #3: An Enterprising Spirit

High potentials are always searching for productive ways to blaze new paths. They are explorers and, as such, take on the challenges of leaving their career comfort zones periodically in order to advance. It might mean a risky move—a tricky international assignment, for instance, or a cross-unit shift that demands an entirely new set of skills. Given high potentials' drive to succeed, you might think they'd be reluctant to take such a chance. But most seem to find that the advantages—the excitement and opportunity—outweigh the risks.

X Factor #4: Dynamic Sensors

Being driven to excel and having an enterprising spirit, combined with the urge to find new approaches, could actually become a recipe for career disaster. High potentials can get derailed for a number of reasons. They may, for instance, be tempted to impulsively accept what seems like a hot opportunity, only to find that it's a break (not a stretch) assignment or that there's no long-term career payoff. Another possibility of derailment comes from a desire to please. High potentials may avoid open disagreement with the boss or resist giving honest, potentially disappointing feedback to a peer. Successful high potentials have well-tuned radar that puts a higher premium on quality results.

Beyond judgment, high potentials possess what we call "dynamic sensors," which enable them to skirt these risks, even if just barely. They have a feel for timing, an ability to quickly read situations, and a nose for opportunity. Their enterprising spirit might otherwise lead them to make foolish decisions, but these sensors help them decide, for example, when to pursue something and when to pull back. High potentials have a knack for being in the right place at the right time.

Anatomy of an X Factor Exemplar

One of the many high potentials we met was Vineet Kapoor, described as a rising star by his bosses at Swiss medical device company Synthes. This more than $3 billion business manufactures and markets implants and biomaterials used in surgery and regeneration of the skeleton and soft tissues.

In school, long before ending up at Synthes, Vineet intended to pursue science and had a passion for improving the lives of people in emerging economies such as India. That basic vision remained with him, but his career took an unexpected path. After college, to the surprise of his peers, he chose accounting in order to gain financial expertise that would serve him well in any business career. He accepted a position with Indian professional services firm A.F. Ferguson, which had a leading portfolio of audit clients (it was eventually acquired by Deloitte in 2004). He then moved to Arthur Andersen (which merged with Ernst & Young) and eventually to KPMG in Gurgaon, India, where his then-boss was charged with leading the India practice. This move initially meant a pay cut for Vineet, but also another chance to learn about building a business.

Vineet recounted other intriguing opportunities that had opened up during his consulting career, when the Sarbanes–Oxley Act became law in the U.S. in 2002. Clients were banging down his door. Although compliance work promised handsome compensation, it didn't match his priorities of learning and effecting large-scale positive change in emerging economies. So Vineet moved to Synthes, where his X factors were evident in spades.

A drive to excel

A drive to succeed can, well, drive some people to the brink. The key is to channel the instinct. So, for instance, Vineet decided he should always think like people one level above him. That meant asking many questions—sometimes to the consternation of his peers and bosses—but he balanced his incessant questioning with an insatiable desire to deliver. Nobody could doubt his commitment to the work and the company, and Vineet's ambition was not a matter of personal triumph. In fact, as country manager for India he created a 150-page book celebrating the contributions of his colleagues and highlighting their common values. It became something of a textbook for the Indian operation at Synthes, and employees found it illuminating. Indeed, it generated so much buzz that some employees who had left the company actually returned because the organization had been energized by it.

Vineet was not driven primarily by a wish to get ahead. His original aspiration was what fueled him. To that end he wrote an 85-page business plan that included a vision for bringing world-class education to all Indian surgeons, including those in remote areas. Synthes's CEO has said that the plan changed how the company looked at India.

A Catalytic Learning Capability

When Vineet traveled to the United States for a Synthes strategy meeting, he stayed on longer to be a "fly on the wall" with the U.S. salespeople. During his stay, Vineet went with them on dozens of sales calls. Having gotten the CEO's attention with his growth strategy, Vineet thought the company would be able to execute it only with the help of more and different employees. He took what he'd learned from the U.S. sales staff to create a new salesperson competency profile for India—one that highlighted entrepreneurship, an attribute he thought would be crucial for delivering on the promise of the Indian market.

An Enterprising Spirit

For Vineet, one of the toughest aspects of career growth was leaving his comfort zone, both professionally and personally. He turned down several opportunities, including one that would have required relocating to the United States. But he eventually took a post as director of strategic initiatives for the Asia Pacific region, a move that forced him to leave India for Singapore. To prepare himself, Vineet agreed to a year of global rotation, spending part of his time in the U.S. corporate office and the rest in the European headquarters in Switzerland. He had to adapt his personal style and develop new strategies. He knew how to lead a team as a country manager, but supporting other country managers in achieving *their* visions was daunting. Vineet loved running his own business and having P&L responsibility; the new job meant playing a support role and

Anatomy of a High Potential

HIGH POTENTIALS ALWAYS deliver strong results, master new types of expertise, and recognize that behavior counts. But it's their intangible X factors that truly distinguish them from the pack.

The Four X Factors of High Potentials

1. Drive to excel
2. Catalytic learning capability
3. Enterprising spirit
4. Dynamic sensors

getting things done through influence instead of direct control.

Dynamic Sensors

High potentials may be resented and envied as well as admired—all of which can be a source of stress. A true high potential understands this and strives to reduce animosity. Vineet certainly cared about how he was perceived. When he was first offered the country manager lead for India, at age 29, he considered turning it down because he thought others might see him as too young or inexperienced. That awareness of others' perceptions is a defining attribute of a high potential.

Developing Your X Factors

The X factors of high potentials not only don't show up in leadership competency models, but also are difficult to teach and learn, particularly in a classroom setting. Nevertheless, you can boost your odds of developing your X factors.

Becoming aware of where you're falling short is the first step. For instance, if you find yourself repeatedly getting blindsided by events, chances are your dynamic sensors aren't very strong. Some people are more attuned to their environment than others, but you can learn to improve your radar by taking simple measures such as listening to others more carefully, observing their reactions to what you say, and refreshing your network of relationships so that it better attunes you to the new businesses and markets your company is pursuing.

Catalytic learning requires an interest in acting, not just learning. Learning without actually changing your behavior is an opportunity wasted. It may be difficult to develop more drive or an enterprising spirit, but with reflection you can begin to be more proactive or take a few more risks. This all speaks to the importance of investing time and energy in self-reflection. You must also recognize the value of seeking advice from a coach or mentor—and of figuring out where an adviser's help ends and your independence begins.

High-Potential Status Has Its Downsides

It's great to be recognized for what you can do and how you might contribute to your company's future, but high-potential status comes at a price. For starters, there's no tenure. People can—and do—fall off the list, and some remove themselves voluntarily or by default because they don't have the time or the passion for the journey. Virtually all companies we surveyed indicated that remaining a high potential is not guaranteed, and

Three C's for CEOs and HR Professionals

AS YOU CULTIVATE YOUR pipeline of high potentials, follow these principles:

> **Be clear** with your people about the skills and behaviors that your organization needs for the future—and about why these characteristics will matter.
>
> **Be consistent** in how you develop talent. Avoid adopting a "development for all" mentality when times are good but then making deep cuts when times are tight.
>
> **Be creative** about the next generation. That marketing manager from Shanghai who doesn't quite fit your mold might be just the talent you need to win in the future.

---

we found that anywhere from 5% to 20% drop off the rolls each year, whether by choice or not.

Among the reasons for losing a spot on the high-potential list are making a poor transition into a new role, diminished performance two years in a row, behavior that's out of line with the company's culture and values, and a significant visible failure. A dramatic fall from grace that stands out in our research involved an executive, whom we'll call Marta, who was in line for the position of chief technology officer at a leading financial services firm.

Marta was an extremely bright high-potential manager with superb technical skills. But she let her smarts get in the way. She didn't want to "waste her time" talking with other senior stakeholders whose clients needed new technology applications. She "knew the right answer" regardless of whether it met clients' needs and expectations. Her dynamic sensors and catalytic learning capability were nowhere to be found. She was intelligent but not wise, and every effort at coaching her failed. Marta was too valuable to be fired, but she was removed from the succession track, which in the end cost her a possible multimillion-dollar payout. She directed the project from a technical standpoint, but her career essentially stalled.

Being singled out for extra developmental attention also can entail sacrifices in your personal life. Some people love to change jobs often, but for others that creates an enormous amount of stress, not to mention tough family-related and other choices. People's expectations of you are high, and colleagues who aren't on the list may secretly, perhaps unconsciously, want you to falter, or even resent you enough to hope you fall from grace.

———————

Getting on a high-potential list can be a significant growth opportunity, so it's not our intention to discourage great managers from aiming for it. However, you need to figure out not just *how* to get on the list, but *why* you want to in the first place. And that means soul-searching. Are you ready for high-potential status? Is it what you really want? If so, the rewards of obtaining it can be huge; if not, then focus on your passions in other ways. Whatever your answer, don't forget: Performance always counts; your behavior matters more and more as you grow; and those X factors are your secret weapons.

DOUGLAS A. READY is the founder and president of ICEDR, a global talent-management research center in Massachusetts. **JAY A. CONGER** is the Henry R. Kravis Research Professor in Leadership Studies at Claremont McKenna College. **LINDA A. HILL** is the Wallace Brett Donham Professor of Business Administration at Harvard Business School.

Originally published in June 2010. Reprint R1006E

Why You Didn't Get That Promotion

by John Beeson

YOU'VE BEEN passed over for a key promotion despite stellar results and glowing reviews. You've asked where you're falling short, but the responses have been vague and unsatisfying, leaving you angry, frustrated, and unsure of how to get ahead. Promotion decisions seem arbitrary and political. What's going on?

In most organizations, promotions are governed by unwritten rules—the often fuzzy, intuitive, and poorly expressed feelings of senior executives regarding individuals' ability to succeed in C-suite positions. As an aspiring executive, you might not know those rules, much less the specific skills you need to develop or demonstrate to follow them. The bottom line: You're left to your own devices in interpreting feedback and finding a way to achieve your career goals.

That's what happened to Ralph Thomas, the vice president of operations for Smith & Mullins's industrial products division, the company's largest operating group. (All names and identifying details in this article are disguised.) He wasn't blindsided by the announcement that Kelly Ferguson had been promoted to senior vice president and general manager for corporate markets—he'd been informed the week before. But Ralph had been a contender, and this was the second time in four years he'd missed out on a division GM job. The first time, Smith & Mullins had hired an outsider who later left the position for a major role at a rival firm.

Ralph always had excellent performance reviews. His 360 results indicated that people loved working for him, and as far as he could tell, managers across the company were beating down the doors to join his group. In terms of execution, his track record was flawless: He and his team had met or surpassed their numbers in each of the past five years. Additionally, they had successfully implemented every major corporate program during that time, and his division had recently been selected to serve as the pilot site for an SAP installation. When he'd learned of these last two GM assignments, he'd also been told that he had a great future with the company and that with a little "seasoning," he'd be ready for advancement. He'd tried several times to get the real scoop on why he hadn't been promoted, only to hear vague comments about improving his "communication skills" and demonstrating more "executive presence" and "leadership." It seemed to him that the company valued people who could look and sound good in the boardroom more than it cared about the year-over-year results of proven performers like himself.

Idea in Brief

Promotions to the C-suite are governed by unwritten rules. If you don't know what they are, you'll be left to your own devices interpreting vague feedback and finding a way to achieve your career goals. Beeson has created a framework to help you identify and address any issues that may be getting in your way. Executive placement decisions hinge on three categories of skills: nonnegotiables, without which you will not be considered for a promotion; deselection factors, which eliminate you as a candidate even if you're otherwise qualified; and core selection factors, which ultimately determine who gets the position. Leadership competency models typically fail to make these distinctions, and most don't spell out how skills should be demonstrated at different levels. In middle management, for instance, teamwork is a vital competency. At more senior levels, the imperatives are to think strategically and to acquire and develop talent. Many unwritten rules are especially elusive because they don't pertain to technical or business knowledge. Rather, they relate to the soft skills that give decision makers an intuitive sense of your potential for success. Complicating matters further, managers and HR professionals often give intentionally vague feedback—not direct constructive criticism—for fear of losing good employees. You'll need to dig deep to get useful input from executives and other colleagues: Project a sincere desire to understand what's holding you back. Ask questions, but don't lobby or argue. Avoid comments or gestures that convey defensiveness, which could cause the other person to clam up or move the conversation to safer territory. And be alert to code words and phrases—such as general observations about the need for "increased leadership ability" or "better communication"—that may mask fundamental issues.

As for Kelly? She'd hired some top people in the past couple of years, but Ralph knew that she had a reputation for being tough on her reports and having "sharp elbows." To Ralph, the promotion wasn't much of an expression of the company's leadership competency model, posted on his office wall: "Display ethics and integrity, envision the future, deliver results, focus on customers, engage in teamwork and collaboration, and develop talent." Ralph bore Kelly no ill will, but it looked as though it was time to update his résumé and rekindle some relationships in his network. Distasteful as it was, testing the job market seemed to be the only way to advance.

The Unwritten Rules

Ralph's situation is surprisingly common, especially among people who aren't politically inclined. Few organizations spell out the criteria for advancement.

Though Ralph had been considered for the GM role both times, in each instance there were bona fide concerns about his readiness. The vague feedback about his communication skills actually alluded to tensions with peers in other units: He could be overly competitive and slow to resolve conflict, whereas Kelly's powers of persuasion allowed her to manage discord and achieve superior results. She was also known for developing talent. Working for her was not for the faint of heart, but she challenged her staff members, and they grew in the process. Ralph didn't recognize that his popularity reflected, in part, his reputation for being a little easy on people—he didn't stretch them to grow and develop. Managers flocking to his unit were often B players who knew he'd cut them some slack. He was luring talent that was good but not great; Kelly was attracting A players who wanted a push. The company's competency model included "develop talent" but didn't specify that having a track record for doing so was nonnegotiable for anyone who wanted to rise beyond Ralph's level.

Under the heading of "leadership" lurked questions regarding Ralph's strategic thinking. He was a go-to guy for implementing corporate initiatives, a master of continuous improvement. But senior management had seen no evidence of his ability to conceive a large-scale change that would produce a quantum leap in performance. Can strategic thinking be developed? That's open to debate, but the fact was that Ralph had always worked for visionaries who never gave him the chance to flex his own strategic muscles, a problem everyone had overlooked.

The information void wasn't a matter of malice; rather, it was due to assumptions that nobody thought to make explicit and an all-too-human reluctance to deliver bad news. Managers and HR professionals often provide intentionally vague feedback for fear of losing a good employee. Further, although most leadership competency models refer in some way to important management skills and attributes, they typically fail to distinguish nice-to-have from nonnegotiable skills.

What's more, such models usually don't spell out how leadership skills should be demonstrated at different levels or how the relative importance of those qualities will change as you rise in the hierarchy. For example, in middle management, teamwork—defined as the ability to maintain cohesion and morale within one's group—is a vital competency. At higher levels, where Ralph hopes to play, it matters less. In fact, at most companies, cohesion tends to fall short at senior levels thanks to rivalry and ego, but teams function pretty well nonetheless. Acquiring and developing talent is the executive's imperative, and teamwork becomes a nice-to-have. Ralph's ability to orchestrate well-functioning teams to complete complex projects, among other skills, had singled him out for previous promotions. But when he was being considered for the GM jobs, strategic thinking became a much higher priority.

Many of the unwritten rules are especially hard to nail down because they don't pertain to technical ability, industry experience, or business knowledge. Rather, they relate to the "soft" skills that combine to give decision makers an intuitive sense of whether a candidate will succeed at the senior level. And, as predictable career paths become more or less extinct, the confusion for people seeking advancement just gets worse.

In my 30 years of experience in and observation of succession planning and executive development at large companies, I've found that the unwritten rules of C-suite placement decisions fall into three categories. *Nonnegotiables* are the fundamental factors without which an executive will not be considered for promotion. *Deselection factors* are characteristics that eliminate an otherwise qualified candidate from consideration. *Core selection factors* are what ultimately dictate promotion decisions. The sidebar "Key Factors in Executive Career Advancement" shows the model I've developed for senior managers. The factors may differ at your company, but the ones highlighted in the exhibit are pretty typical.

Ralph passes the test on the nonnegotiables and the deselection factors but falls short on several core selection factors, like thinking strategically, building a strong executive team, and having the organization savvy to work effectively across internal boundaries. If Smith & Mullins made a list of such factors available to its executives, along with a dose of constructive feedback, Ralph would probably be able to see where he needs to devote his energies.

But since it doesn't, Ralph has to tease out the underlying issues. Although he periodically gets feedback from 360s, such reviews—unless combined with confidential face-to-face interviews by a third party—are rarely sufficient to illuminate the core reasons behind a stalled career.

One obvious way to get insight is to approach your boss and colleagues directly for their opinions, though their input might be of limited use. They may not be straight with you, and their perspectives may differ from those of the most senior decision makers. For additional information, you might have a conversation with your former manager or your boss's boss. Try to contact the highest-level manager who is knowledgeable about your work and with whom you have a positive relationship, so your approach seems natural and appropriate. (Caveat: Don't go behind your boss's back. He or she should know about any contact with other executives and what your intentions are.) For the reasons stated above, you'll probably have to dig a little to get useful information. That's not easy, so let's take a closer look at how you can go about having a truly constructive conversation.

How to Ask, How to Listen

Getting past executives' reluctance to provide direct and difficult feedback is tricky. When asking for input, project a sincere desire to understand what's holding you back—and avoid appearing to lobby or argue. Your core question should be "What skills and capabilities do I need to demonstrate in order to be a strong candidate for higher levels of responsibility at some point in the future?"

Get into active-listening mode. Any comment or body language that conveys defensiveness will most likely cause the other person to either clam up or move the conversation to easier (and vaguer) territory—such as the need for more "seasoning" that Ralph kept hearing about. Ask clarifying questions, but don't challenge the content. (You can attempt to correct factual errors with the right person later; this isn't the time.) Be alert to code words and phrases masking fundamental issues— general observations about the need for "increased leadership ability" or "better teamwork" or "improved communication."

For instance, a manager I'll call Terry was told by her boss that she needed to improve her leadership skills before she'd be eligible for her next promotion. She was managing multiple initiatives, and her teams were functioning effectively; she didn't see how to improve her leadership except by taking on more projects. Fortunately, she had worked for her boss's manager earlier in her career and could set up a meeting. In a series of probing questions, she asked the manager to help her define what "better leadership" would be in her case. She discovered that in her dedication she in fact had been doing herself a disservice. She'd been given an ever-increasing number of projects because of her superior organizational and people-management skills and her ability to stay on top of details. However, senior managers were concerned that she was maxed out by her personal involvement in every initiative and wanted to see that she could delegate more and create processes and systems that would ensure flawless execution without so much direct supervision.

In response she put considerable effort into rethinking how she spent her time: which issues she should be involved in personally, which she could—with some coaching—learn to delegate to others, and what kinds of meetings and reports would allow her to stay as close to projects as was needed. She revamped her team's staff meeting and the level of preparation required. She also designated a direct report as chief of staff to follow up on deadlines and alert her to situations that required her intervention. Terry admits that it was initially difficult to extricate herself from the details on some projects and confesses to poring over the status reports submitted by the staff. But with practice she got better at letting go. A year later she was promoted to lead a large operational unit.

Things don't always work out so well. Ed, a highly proficient finance manager, had advanced quickly because of his technical knowledge but recently missed out on several key promotions. His boss told him not to worry, everything was fine. Still, Ed met with his unit's

Key Factors in Executive Career Advancement

Nonnegotiables

Factors that are absolutely necessary for you to be a contender

- Demonstrating consistently strong performance
- Displaying ethics, integrity, and character
- Being driven to lead and to assume higher levels of responsibility

Deselection Factors

Characteristics that prevent you from being considered as a serious candidate

- Having weak interpersonal skills
- Treating others with insensitivity or abrasiveness
- Putting self-interest above company good
- Holding a narrow, parochial perspective on the business and the organization

Core Selection Factors

Capabilities that breed others' confidence in your ability to succeed at the senior executive level

- Setting direction and thinking strategically; spotting marketplace trends and developing a winning strategy that differentiates the company

HR manager, who advised him to improve his communication skills. This confused him; he took pride in his ability to write and speak clearly and devoted a lot of time to communicating with his staff. At the suggestion of the HR manager, he met with three peers to get their opinions. All three were hesitant to offer their opinions

- Building and continually upgrading a strong executive team; having a "nose for talent"; establishing an adequate level of team cohesion

- Managing implementation without getting involved at too low a level of detail; defining a set of roles, processes, and measures to ensure that things get done reliably

- Building the capacity for innovation and change; knowing when new ways of doing business are required; having the courage, tolerance for risk, and change-management skills to bring new ideas to fruition

- Getting things done across internal boundaries (lateral management); demonstrating organization savvy; influencing and persuading colleagues; dealing well with conflict

- Growing and developing as an executive; soliciting and responding to feedback; adjusting leadership style in light of experience

until Ed probed specifically for examples of poor communication on his part. It turned out that he was right; his basic communication skills were fine. Rather, the underlying issue lay with his ability to listen and to be flexible. Colleagues complained that he tended to get locked into his own opinions, that he lacked openness to other perspectives and shut down creative alternatives. Some considered him arrogant.

Overall, his peers recommended that Ed spend more time discussing his plans with them and soliciting input. Unfortunately, Ed saw this as "politics" and energy that would be diverted from getting things done. Exacerbating the situation was the fact that Ed's boss was encouraging him to drive the implementation of a new corporate policy that Ed's peers found onerous. When his boss took a new position within the company, Ed suddenly felt vulnerable. Using his extensive industry network, he quickly found another position with a well-regarded firm but ended up leaving his new job after only nine months. The official reason was that Ed was not a cultural fit in a highly collaborative environment. In reality Ed's peers at the new company complained that he was a know-it-all who tried to sell major initiatives to his boss without taking the time to understand how the organization worked and what internal customers needed.

If you are having trouble decoding the feedback you receive, try asking at the end of each session, "What one or two things—above all others—would most build confidence in my ability to succeed at higher levels within the organization?" As long as the other person answers honestly, this question tends to circumvent vagueness and separate the wheat from the chaff.

Keep in mind that changing deep-seated perceptions about you, formed over years, requires visible and consistent effort—which is why it is typically best to focus on one or two key areas of development. Think through whether your current position provides you with a platform to demonstrate needed skills. Ralph, for instance, may need to move to a position where his breakthrough thinking isn't preempted by a visionary boss. Alternatively, he may find ample opportunities to exhibit strategic thinking in his current role—if he is aggressive and creative in pursuing them and his boss gives him room to experiment.

Although this type of development isn't easy, the payoff can be huge for both the individual and the organization. Employees like Ralph learn what's really holding them back, and companies like Smith & Mullins get a deeper and better bench.

JOHN BEESON is the principal of Beeson Consulting.

Originally published in June 2009. Reprint R0906L

Why Men Still Get More Promotions Than Women

by Herminia Ibarra, Nancy M. Carter, and Christine Silva

NATHALIE (all names in this article are disguised), a senior marketing manager at a multinational consumer goods company and a contender for chairman in her country, was advised by her boss to raise her profile locally. An excellent intracompany network wouldn't be enough to land her the new role, he told her; she must also become active in events and associations in her region. Recently matched with a high-level mentor through a companywide program, she had barely completed the lengthy prework assigned for that when she received an invitation to an exclusive executive-training program for high potentials—for which she was asked to fill out more self-assessments and career-planning documents. "I'd been here for 12 years, and nothing happened," observes Nathalie. "Now I am being mentored to death."

Amy, a midlevel sales manager for the same firm, struggles with a similar problem: "My mentor's idea of a development plan is how many external and internal meetings I can get exposure to, what presentations I can go to and deliver, and what meetings I can travel to," she says. "I just hate these things that add work. I hate to say it, but I am so busy. I have three kids. On top of that, what my current boss really wants me to do is to focus on 'breakthrough thinking,' and I agree. I am going to be in a wheelchair by the time I get to be vice president, because they are going to drill me into the ground with all these extra-credit projects."

With turnover sky-high in the company's fast-growing Chinese market, Julie, a much-valued finance manager with growth potential, has likewise undergone intensive mentoring—and she worries that she may be getting caught betwixt and between. When she was nominated for a high-potential program, her boss complained that the corporate team was interfering with the mentoring operation he was already running in the region. Julie also took part in a less formal scheme pairing junior and senior finance leaders. "I'd prefer to be involved in the corporate program because it is more high-profile," says Julie, "but it all adds up to a lot of mentoring."

Nathalie, Amy, and Julie are not atypical. As companies continue to see their pipelines leak at mid-to-senior levels even though they've invested considerable time and resources in mentors and developmental opportunities, they are actively searching for ways to

Idea in Brief

Though companies now invest heavily in mentoring and developing their best female talent, all that attention doesn't translate into promotions. A Catalyst survey of over 4,000 high potentials shows that more women than men have mentors—yet women are paid $4,600 less in their first post-MBA jobs, hold lower-level positions, and feel less career satisfaction. To better understand why, the authors conducted in-depth interviews with 40 participants in a mentoring program at a large multinational. All mentoring is not created equal, they discovered. Only sponsorship involves advocacy for advancement. The interviews and survey alike indicate that, compared with their male peers, high potential women are overmentored, undersponsored, and not advancing in their organizations. Without sponsorship, women not only are less likely than men to be appointed to top roles but may also be more reluctant to go for them. Organizations such as Deutsche Bank, Unilever, Sodexo, and IBM Europe have established sponsorship programs to facilitate the promotion of high-potential women. Programs that get results clarify and communicate their goals, match sponsors and mentees on the basis of those goals, coordinate corporate and regional efforts, train sponsors, and hold those sponsors accountable.

retain their best female talent. In a 2010 World Economic Forum report on corporate practices for gender diversity in 20 countries, 59% of the companies surveyed say they offer internally led mentoring and networking programs, and 28% say they have women-specific programs. But does all this effort translate into actual promotions and appointments for both sexes?

The numbers suggest not. A 2008 Catalyst survey of more than 4,000 full-time-employed men and women—high potentials who graduated from top MBA programs worldwide from 1996 to 2007—shows that the women are paid $4,600 less in their first post-MBA jobs, occupy lower-level management positions, and have significantly less career satisfaction than their male counterparts with the same education. That's also the case when we take into account factors such as their industry, prior work experience, aspirations, and whether they have children. (For more findings, see Nancy M. Carter and Christine Silva, "Women in Management: Delusions of Progress," HBR March 2010.) Yet among that same group, more women than men report having mentors. If the women are being mentored so thoroughly, why aren't they moving into higher management positions?

To better understand what is going on, we conducted in-depth interviews with 40 high-potential men and women (including Nathalie, Amy, and Julie) who were selected by their large multinational company to participate in its high-level mentoring program. We asked about the hurdles they've faced as they've moved into more-senior roles, as well as what kinds of help and support they've received for their transitions. We also analyzed the 2008 survey to uncover any differences in how men and women are mentored and in the effects of their mentoring on advancement. Last, we compared those data with the results of a 2010 survey of the same population, in which we asked participants to report on promotions and lateral moves since 2008.

All mentoring is not created equal, we discovered. There is a special kind of relationship—called sponsorship—in which the mentor goes beyond giving feedback and advice and uses his or her influence with senior executives to advocate for the mentee. Our interviews and surveys alike suggest that high-potential women are overmentored and undersponsored relative to their male peers—and that they are not advancing in their organizations. Furthermore, without sponsorship, women not only are less likely than men to be appointed to top roles but may also be more reluctant to go for them.

Why Mentoring Fails Women

Although more women than men in the 2008 Catalyst survey report having mentors, the women's mentors have less organizational clout. We find this to be true even after controlling for the fact that women start in lower-level positions post-MBA. That's a real disadvantage, the study shows, because the more senior the mentor, the faster the mentee's career advancement. Despite all the effort that has gone into developing the women since 2008, the follow-up survey in 2010 reveals that the men have received 15% more promotions. The two groups have had similar numbers of lateral moves (same-level job assignments in different functions, designed to give high potentials exposure to various parts of the business). But men were receiving promotions after the lateral moves; for the women, the moves were offered in lieu of advancement.

Of course, the ultimate test of the power of mentoring would be to show that its presence during the 2008 survey is a statistically significant predictor of promotion by the time of the 2010 survey. That's true for the men but not for the women. Though women may be getting support and guidance, mentoring relationships aren't leading to nearly as many promotions for them as for men.

The survey findings are echoed in our interviews: Men and women alike say they get valuable career advice from their mentors, but it's mostly men who describe being sponsored. Many women explain how mentoring relationships have helped them understand themselves, their preferred styles of operating, and ways they might need to change as they move up the leadership pipeline. By contrast, men tell stories about how their bosses and informal mentors have helped them plan their moves and take charge in new roles, in addition to endorsing their authority publicly. As one male mentee recounts, in a typical comment: "My boss said, 'You are ready for a general management job. You can do it. Now we need to find you a job: What are the tricks we need to figure out? You have to talk to this person and to that one and that one.' They are all executive committee members. My boss was a network type of a person. . . . Before he left, he put me in touch with the head of supply chain, which is how I managed to get this job."

Not only do the women report few examples of this kind of endorsement; they also share numerous stories about how they've had to fight with their mentors to be viewed as ready for the next role.

Paradoxically, just when women are most likely to need sponsorship—as they shoot for the highest-level jobs—they may be least likely to get it. Women are still perceived as "risky" appointments for such roles by often male-dominated committees. In a study

Are women as likely as men to get mentoring? Yes.

THEY'RE ACTUALLY MORE SO: In the 2008 Catalyst survey, 83% of women and 76% of men say they've had at least one mentor at some point in their careers. Indeed, 21% of women say they've had four or more mentors, compared with 15% of men.

of top-performing CEOs, for instance, the women were nearly twice as likely as the men to have been hired from outside the company (see Morten T. Hansen, Herminia Ibarra, and Urs Peyer, "The Best-Performing CEOs in the World," HBR January–February 2010). That finding suggests that women are less likely to emerge as winners in their firms' own CEO tournaments.

Sponsorship That Works

Impatient with the speed at which women are reaching the top levels, many leading-edge companies we work with are converging on a new set of strategies to ensure that high-potential women are sponsored for the most-senior posts. Those principles can make all the difference between a sponsorship program that gets results and one that simply looks great on paper.

Clarify and communicate the intent of the program.
It's hard to do a good job of both mentoring and sponsoring within the same program. Often the best mentors—those who provide caring and altruistic advice and counseling—are not the highfliers who have

Does mentoring provide the same career benefits to men and women? No.

AMONG SURVEY PARTICIPANTS who had active mentoring relationships in 2008, fully 72% of the men had received one or more promotions by 2010, compared with 65% of the women.

the influence to pull people up through the system. Employees expecting one form of support can be very disappointed when they get the other. And companies hoping to do A can find themselves with a program that instead does B. To prevent such problems, they need to clearly define what they're trying to accomplish.

At Deutsche Bank, for example, internal research revealed that female managing directors who left the firm to work for competitors were not doing so to improve their work/life balance. Rather, they'd been offered bigger jobs externally, ones they weren't considered for internally. Deutsche Bank responded by creating a sponsorship program aimed at assigning more women to critical posts. It paired mentees with executive committee members to increase the female talent pool's exposure to the committee and ensure that the women had influential advocates for promotion. Now, one-third of the participants are in larger roles than they were in a year ago, and another third are deemed ready by senior management and HR to take on broader responsibilities.

Do men and women have the same kinds of mentors? No.

IN 2008, 78% OF MEN were actively mentored by a CEO or another senior executive, compared with 69% of women.

More women than men had junior-level mentors: 7% of women were mentored by a nonmanager or a first-level manager, compared with 4% of men.

Though both groups had more male than female mentors on balance, 36% of women had female mentors, whereas only 11% of men did.

Select and match sponsors and high-potential women in light of program goals.

When the objective of a program is career advancement for high potentials, mentors and sponsors are typically selected on the basis of position power. When the goal is personal development, matches are made to increase the likelihood of frequent contact and good chemistry.

Unilever has established a program with the explicit objective of promoting more high-potential women to the firm's most-senior levels. The two key criteria for selecting the sponsors, all members of Unilever's senior ranks, are experience in areas where the high potentials have developmental gaps, and presence at the table when the appointment decisions get made. Given the company's international scope and matrix organization, this means that many of the women do not live and work in the same location as their sponsors. So some don't spend much face-to-face time with sponsors, but they do have advocates at promotion time.

Coordinate efforts and involve direct supervisors.

Centrally run mentoring programs that sidestep direct bosses can inadvertently communicate that diversity is an HR problem that requires no effort from the front lines.

Coordination of corporate and local efforts is especially important when it comes to senior-level participants in whom companies invest significantly. Effective sponsorship does not stand alone but is one facet of a comprehensive program that includes performance evaluation, training and development, and succession planning—all of which add up to more than the sum of the parts. The Deutsche Bank sponsorship program for female managing directors, for instance, is one piece of a highly tailored initiative that also involves leadership evaluations, external coaches, and leadership workshops.

Train sponsors on the complexities of gender and leadership.

Good sponsorship requires a set of skills and sensibilities that most companies' star executives do not necessarily possess. When you layer on top some of the complexities of sponsor relationships between senior men and junior women, you easily have a recipe for misunderstanding. The strategies and tactics that helped the men progress in their careers may not be appealing or even feasible for the women.

A classic case is the challenge of developing a credible leadership style in a context where most of the successful role models are male. One of the women in

Do men and women get their mentors in the same way? Yes.

MOST MEN AND WOMEN—67% of the groups combined—found their mentors on their own, relying on personal networks. Just 18% of women and 16% of men formed their mentoring relationships with the help of formal programs.

our research describes the problem like this: "My mentor advised me that I should pay more attention to my strategic influencing skills . . . but often he suggests I do things that totally contradict my personality." The behavioral styles that are most valued in traditionally masculine cultures—and most used as indicators of "potential"—are often unappealing or unnatural for high-potential women, whose sense of authenticity can feel violated by the tacit leadership requirements.

A further complexity is the famed "double bind" examined in Alice H. Eagly and Linda L. Carli's book *Through the Labyrinth* (Harvard Business Review Press, 2007) and in the 2007 Catalyst research report "The Double-Bind Dilemma for Women in Leadership." Here's the problem, in short: The assertive, authoritative, dominant behaviors that people associate with leadership are frequently deemed less attractive in women. Male mentors who have never faced this dilemma themselves may be hard-pressed to provide useful advice. As one of our interview participants describes, even well-intended mentors have trouble helping women navigate the fine line between being "not aggressive enough" or "lacking in presence" and

Does having formal versus informal mentoring make any difference in terms of promotions? Yes.

WOMEN WHO HAD FOUND MENTORS through formal programs had received more promotions by 2010 than women who had found mentors on their own (by a ratio of almost three to two).

Among all participants who had found mentors on their own, the men received more promotions than the women (again, by a ratio of almost three to two).

For more on how companies are providing sponsorship, go to www.catalyst.org/publication/413/mentoring-sponsorship.

being "too aggressive" or "too controlling." She explains the challenge of dealing with conflicting expectations from two different bosses: "My old boss told me, 'If you want to move up, you have to change your style. You are too brutal, too demanding, too tough, too clear, and not participative enough.' My new boss is different: He drives performance, values speed. Now I am told, 'You have to be more demanding.' I was really working on being more indirect, but now I will try to combine the best of both."

Male sponsors can be taught to recognize such gender-related dilemmas. Women in Sodexo's reciprocal-mentoring program, for example, have been promoted at higher rates than other high potential women at the company, in part because the senior male mentors serve as career sponsors and (thanks to the upward mentoring) learn to manage their unconscious biases.

Hold sponsors accountable.

To fully reap the benefits of sponsorship, companies must hold sponsors accountable. At IBM Europe, a sponsorship program designed for senior women below the executive level aims to promote selected participants within one year. Sponsors, all vice presidents or general managers, are charged with making sure that participants are indeed ready within a year. So they work hard to raise the women's profiles, talk up the candidates to decision makers, and find the high potentials internal projects that will fill in their skills gaps and make them promotable. Failure to obtain a promotion is viewed as a failure of the sponsor, not of the candidate.

Although our data show that formal programs can be quite effective in getting women promoted, a potential pitfall is their fixed duration. Sponsors typically declare victory and move on after their high potentials advance—just when they need help to successfully take charge in their new roles. We know of no programs designed to shore up participants past promotion and through the "first 100 days" in the new position. With that extra bit of attention, sponsors could help deliver not just promotions but strong transitions.

Although the women we interviewed all come from the same company, the trends there mirror those at many other firms we've worked with and observed. And the survey responses, gathered from men and women at hundreds of firms, also provide strong evidence for gender difference in mentoring outcomes.

Mentors and Sponsors: How They Differ

COMPANIES NEED TO MAKE A SHARPER distinction between mentoring and sponsorship. Mentors offer "psychosocial" support for personal and professional development, plus career help that includes advice and coaching, as Boston University's Kathy Kram explains in her pioneering research. Only sponsors actively advocate for advancement.

"Classical mentoring" (ideal but rare) combines psychosocial and career support. Usually, though, workers get one or the other—or if they get both, it's from different sources.

Analysis of hundreds of studies shows that people derive more satisfaction from mentoring but need sponsorship. Without sponsorship, a person is likely to be overlooked for promotion, regardless of his or her competence and performance—particularly at mid-career and beyond, when competition for promotions increases.

Mentors

- Can sit at any level in the hierarchy
- Provide emotional support, feedback on how to improve, and other advice

More sponsoring may lead to more and faster promotions for women, but it is not a magic bullet: There is still much to do to close the gap between men's and women's advancement. Some improvements—such as supportive bosses and inclusive cultures—are a lot harder to mandate than formal mentoring programs but essential if those programs are to have their intended effects. Clearly, however, the critical first step is to stop

- Serve as role models
- Help mentees learn to navigate corporate politics
- Strive to increase mentees' sense of competence and self-worth
- Focus on mentees' personal and professional development

Sponsors

- Must be senior managers with influence
- Give protégés exposure to other executives who may help their careers
- Make sure their people are considered for promising opportunities and challenging assignments
- Protect their protégés from negative publicity or damaging contact with senior executives
- Fight to get their people promoted

overmentoring and start accountable sponsoring for both sexes.

HERMINIA IBARRA is the Cora Chaired Professor of Leadership and Learning at Insead in France and the author of *Working Identity: Unconventional Strategies for Reinventing Your Career* (Harvard Business Review

Press, 2003). **NANCY M. CARTER** is the vice president of research at Catalyst, which works with businesses to expand opportunities for women. **CHRISTINE SILVA** is a director of research at Catalyst.

Originally published in September 2010. Reprint R1009F

Five Ways to Bungle a Job Change

by Boris Groysberg and Robin Abrahams

THE AVERAGE BABY BOOMER will switch jobs 10 times, according to the U.S. Bureau of Labor Statistics. The worker as free agent—a concept popularized in the 1990s—remains a reality regardless of economic conditions, making it incumbent on all of us to take greater control of our own careers. The corporate ladder is still being disassembled like a Jenga tower, and even the CEO position is no longer a terminus. As one independent financier we interviewed put it, "[T]here are no final destinations. [Your career] is a process of continuous development."

But while job moves are just about inevitable, they are seldom easy and nearly always emotionally fraught—and too often they lead to a noticeable decline in performance, in both the short and the long term. For instance, in previous research we found that star equities analysts moving to new investment banks experienced drops in performance that lasted as long as five years. People who switch organizations—whether they're wide receivers changing football teams or general managers going to new companies—all face similar problems. It's not just about the learning curve. Moves of all kinds entail significant internal and external challenges and transaction costs: upheaval in your home and social life; potential relocation expenses; adjustments to new cultural and political norms; navigation of unclear expectations; and the need to learn a new canon, skill set, and jargon.

Debating the merits of a particular offer might seem like a luxury when jobs are scarce. And of course there are times when you have no choice but to accept a less-than-perfect fit for financial reasons. Even so, a job is never just a job. This is your *career* we're talking about. The occasional misstep can be forgiven, but a careful and conscious assessment of the risks and realities will help you avoid making too many mistakes or ones that amount to a major setback.

The Most Common Missteps

To identify the most frequent job-hopping errors, we analyzed data from three research streams: a survey of executive search consultants, a survey of HR heads at multinational companies, and interviews with C-level executives around the world. (See "About Our Research.")

The job-change mistakes we outline in this article are by far the ones most commonly cited by the search consultants; the themes are echoed in the HR heads' survey

Idea in Brief

The average baby boomer switches jobs 10 times in his or her career. Though such moves are just about inevitable, they're seldom easy—and they often lead to a noticeable decline in both short- and long-term performance. That's because people make them for the wrong reasons. Drawing on an extensive survey of executive search consultants, as well as surveys of HR heads and interviews with C-level executives around the world, the authors have identified senior managers' five most common career missteps: not doing enough research, leaving for money, going "from" rather than "to," overestimating yourself, and thinking short term. These mistakes follow predictable patterns and persist throughout the course of a career; they're often a direct result of psychological, social, and time pressures. What if you do take the wrong job? The authors' research indicates that you should cut your losses and leave. But fleeing to another bad situation is not the answer. Make your next move strategically—and wherever you are in the search process, don't hesitate to go down another road when it becomes evident that a certain kind of change wouldn't be right.

comments and in the executives' stories about their best and worst decisions. The mistakes are: not doing enough research, leaving for money, going "from" rather than "to," overestimating yourself, and thinking short term. They follow predictable patterns and persist throughout the course of a career.

These mistakes are not independent of one another; they play out as a system of maladaptive behaviors, dissatisfaction, unrealistic hopes, ill-considered moves, and more dissatisfaction. Fixating on money, for instance, can obscure the need for research. Overestimating yourself can cause you to ignore a bad fit—a problem that research might have helped you anticipate. Some

About Our Research

FOR THIS ARTICLE, we conducted a survey of 400 executive search consultants from more than 50 industries, interviews with more than 500 C-level executives in 40 countries, and a survey of HR heads at 15 multinational companies.

The search consultants had extensive experience placing the best and brightest: In our sample, 67% had 10-plus years of experience, and 70% recruited for stars at the senior-executive level or higher. We asked the consultants to name the most common mistakes people make when contemplating a job change and the reasons for those mistakes. We posed similar questions to the HR heads. The interviews with executives were conducted by students in Boris Groysberg's 2008 class Managing Human Capital.

The consultants referred to a total of 738 mistakes. The top five kinds discussed in this article represent nearly two-thirds of them: We had 127 references to not doing enough research, 117 to leaving for money, 104 to going "from" rather than "to," 76 to overestimating yourself, and 60 to thinking short term.

The smaller survey of HR heads matched the consultants' feedback almost perfectly. Out of a total of 15 responses, not doing enough research was mentioned five times; leaving for money and going "from" rather than "to," three times each; overestimating yourself, twice; and thinking short term, once.

job seekers make all five mistakes at once: Because they overvalue themselves, they feel unjustly treated at year-end review time and leave for the first company that promises a signing bonus, without doing due diligence on the firm's long-term prospects.

The executives we surveyed and spoke to were not young, untested managers. We zeroed in on seasoned individuals (mostly in the C-suite) with substantial experience making hiring decisions of their own at the very highest levels. But, as one search consultant reminded us, many successful people haven't looked for a job for years—sometimes decades—and thus are surprisingly ignorant about job-market realities. In the words of another consultant, "They assume that companies will be as flexible about having them learn new areas of business as they were when they were young." They have unrealistic expectations about how long it will take to find a job, and if they're high up in the hierarchy, it may have been some time since they received truly honest feedback about their strengths and weaknesses. That's one reason they stumble into such predictable traps. (The blame doesn't fall solely on the recruits, though. Companies chase these stars, hoping to simply plug them into an existing org chart. Too often, they are minimally strategic in their selection and even less strategic in integrating their new hires.)

Mistake 1: Not doing enough research.

Search consultants told us that job hunters neglect due diligence in four important areas.

First, they often don't do their homework on the job-market realities for their industry or function. Since they're not fully informed, they have unrealistic expectations when it comes to the search.

Second, they don't pay enough attention to a potential employer's financial stability and market position. Executives who would scrutinize the balance sheet of any firm they might acquire nevertheless assume that companies offering them a job must be on solid ground. Yet plenty of businesses will hire for senior jobs even when they know there's trouble ahead, so it's up to the applicant to assess how likely it is that the new job will still exist in six months.

Third, executives fail to consider cultural fit. Although hiring managers are supposed to attend to that, they often don't—and it's the new hire who will suffer most if the fit is a poor one.

Fourth, recruits assume that the official job title and description accurately reflect the role. But companies have been known to sweeten a title to attract top talent. Additionally, in a badly managed organization, people may find themselves in ill-defined jobs that have little relationship to their formal titles. One executive described his worst career move as leaving one company for a much smaller firm, where he was given the CFO title even though the bulk of his duties were really those of a COO. He found it hard to establish the credibility he needed to get the job done, given the misalignment of his tasks and title. Job candidates frequently fail to press potential employers for such specifics, including how their performance will be measured. Without that information, the success of any move depends on the luck of the draw.

Mistake 2: Leaving for money.
It's easy to fall for a financially attractive offer. Search consultants told us that executives contemplating a job change rank income fourth or fifth in terms of importance but bump it to first place when making

their decision. Our executive interviewees occasionally owned up to this error. Here's how the vice president of talent and engagement at an international casino company characterized his own move based on pay: "I was doing the identical role for $10K more, but leaving behind the relationships and connections was just not worth it in hindsight." Excessive focus on money is a frequently cited reason for inadequate research. "Opportunity for advancement and more money overrides the need to pursue core information," said one search consultant.

Mistake 3: Going "from" rather than "to."

Often, job seekers have become so unhappy with their present positions that they are desperate to get out. Instead of planning their career moves, they lurch from one place to the next, applying artificial urgency to the job hunt rather than waiting for the right offer. Candidates not only skimp on research in the belief that the grass has to be greener elsewhere but also fail to look strategically at their current companies for opportunities that might still exist for them.

Mistake 4: Overestimating yourself.

According to one search consultant, people "believe they contribute more than they actually do and undervalue the strengths of their organization in helping them achieve their objectives." Job seekers, we found, tend to have an unrealistic view of their skills, their prospects, and occasionally their culpability. They often can't identify the sources of success and failure at their existing jobs. Candidates are "looking at the current company as being the problem and not acknowledging that they themselves may be a part of the problem," one consultant explained. Another put it this way: "People fail to be realistic sometimes [and] to be self-critical, and [they therefore think] that external circumstances and environments have more to do with their frustrations or failures than their own issues."

Their excessively optimistic view of themselves leads them to underestimate how long a job search will take and what the switching costs will be. Such job seekers also overestimate the salary they can command and their capacity to deal with the challenges of the new position—particularly the difficulty of creating change in a large organization. This last error resonated with many of the executives we interviewed. One software CFO regretted taking a job at a large multinational, where it was "so much bigger, more unwieldy, difficult to make an impact, and impersonal," he says. "No matter what I did, it didn't make a difference."

Mistake 5: Thinking short term.
Having a short-term perspective can feed into each of the other four mistakes. For instance, if you overestimate yourself, you may believe you deserve rewards now, not in five years. Leaving a firm because of money and going "from" rather than "to" are both overly influenced by immediate information and considerations. "How much money can I make right now?" the executive wonders. "How can I escape an unpleasant work environment?" Still, many of the search consultants

rated short-term thinking as a serious career misstep in its own right—citing it separately, not just including it as a footnote to the other mistakes.

Making Moves Under Pressure

Job seekers' mistakes aren't random. All of us feel certain psychological, social, and time pressures that can lead to any of the five we've described. Though nobody is immune, we can ask questions of ourselves and others to help ameliorate these pressures' effects.

Psychological Pressure

We are all motivated to maintain a sense of psychological safety by nurturing a positive self-image, by looking at the world as a knowable and predictable place, and by avoiding risk. This can lead to an overestimation of the self and to a habit of attending only to information that bolsters your existing beliefs. Psychologists call this selective attention "confirmation bias," and it can play havoc with a strategic job search. A hiring company presumably wants to present itself in the most flattering light, and if a candidate is motivated to move, he or she will be more than willing to see only the bright side.

Our self-protective desires go beyond the ego. We also seek to protect our material well-being by minimizing losses. Because what people give up when they leave a job is so clear (at the very worst, it's still the devil you know), excessive focus on short-term rewards and money may be a way of hedging against long-term risks that cannot really be evaluated.

Here are the fundamental questions to ask through every step of the job-change process: "What if I'm wrong? What is the evidence that this new company would be a good fit?" Do at least as much research on a company you're planning to join as you would on a company you're planning to buy stock in. Develop alternative scenarios. Consider how you'd feel about your present job if your boss left, for instance, or if the company secured an enticing new client. And rethink self-serving interpretations of events—how, for example, did your colleagues contribute to your success? This is difficult work, and it's tough to manage by yourself. Many of the executives we interviewed rely on a mentor, network, or personal "board of directors" to provide this kind of reality check.

Social Pressure

Awkward social situations can trigger fight-or-flight instincts, putting strategic thinking squarely on the back burner—and they frequently lead people to make "from" rather than "to" decisions. The CFO of a marketing agency recounts such a situation from his own career, in which he changed jobs rather than have an awkward conversation or two: "Even though I enjoyed the company and had a great relationship with the CFO, I never spoke with him about my concerns before quitting. In retrospect, I realize that the CFO could have been instrumental in advancing my career within that company. If I had stayed . . . I could see myself being very happy and secure today."

Stress management techniques like yoga and meditation can help alleviate this kind of social anxiety. So can rehearsing difficult conversations, alone or with a partner. By practicing clear communication, and by repeatedly restating your concerns, you can suppress your emotional reactions and remain rational in an actual conversation. Through candid conversations with colleagues or your boss, you might be able to redeem your current job rather than make an ill-advised change.

If you are seriously contemplating a move, don't be afraid to ask tough questions at a job interview. When an interviewer can't handle direct, relevant questions, what does that say about the corporate culture?

Social discomfort intimidates us far beyond its power to harm us; as is widely known, most people rank public speaking as a fear greater than death. Deconstructing such irrational fear can help free you from the social pressures that may lead you to make hurried, unhappy career moves.

Time Pressure

A hasty job change, made with insufficient information, is inherently compromised. When under time pressure, people tend to make certain predictable mistakes. They focus on readily available details like salary and job title instead of raising deeper questions, and they set their sights on the immediate future, either discounting or misreading the long term. Many also have an egocentric bias, thinking only of what affects them directly and ignoring the larger context.

Nonetheless, a career move will always involve some time pressure. To manage it, one COO in our study says he always keeps an ear to the ground with respect to industry trends, both in the U.S. and abroad. He explains that this is a way to stay ahead of the curve when it comes to career decisions. But no matter how well informed you are, you need strategies to jar yourself out of traditional ways of thinking and to make sure you aren't heeding only the nearest, loudest, quickest source of information. With the help of your mentor or network, create a list of unknowns. Engage in counter-factual-thinking exercises: Consider whether you'd take the new job if the salary were the same as your current pay. Plot the most likely three-year trajectory at each company, working out the most optimistic and pessimistic scenarios. What decision would be right in each situation?

What if you do take the wrong job? The executives we interviewed were unanimous in their views: Cut your losses and move on. Fleeing to another bad situation is not the answer, though. We suggest making your next move strategically—and wherever you are in the search process, don't hesitate to go down another road if it becomes evident that a certain kind of change wouldn't be right.

Perhaps the best protection against career-management mistakes is self-awareness. It's a broad concept, encompassing not only an understanding of your career-relevant strengths and weaknesses but also insight into the kinds of mistakes you are prone to make. It involves knowing how to correct for those tendencies, how others perceive you, when to consult a trusted mentor or network, what elements of a job make it truly satisfying for you, and what constitutes a healthy work-life balance.

BORIS GROYSBERG is an associate professor and **ROBIN ABRAHAMS** is a research associate at Harvard Business School.

Originally published in January 2010. Reprint R1001M

The Right Way to Be Fired

by Laurence J. Stybel and Maryanne Peabody

EVEN IN THE BEST OF TIMES, executives get fired, and in the worst, they get fired with disquieting frequency. Indeed, as the economy softens, you only have to glance at the newspaper to see layoffs left, right, and center, mainly to cut costs. You can be a top performer today and still lose your job. The question is: Can you lose it the right way?

For 22 years, we have worked closely with more than 500 senior executives in dozens of industries to manage their careers in good times and in bad. Over and over, we have observed how executives react to being fired or laid off. The majority handle termination with dignity, even elegance. They negotiate handsome severance packages, part with their employers on amicable terms, and position themselves for their next assignments. Yet some executives take actions that subsequently backfire, setting the stage for difficulty in procuring new jobs—and even destroying their careers.

What differentiates fired employees who make the best of their situations from those who do not? One answer is mind-set. Virtually every executive feels shock and anger upon losing a job, but those who rebound swiftly have usually absorbed what we call an "assignment mentality"; they see each job as a stepping-stone, a temporary career-building project. That's good, because most corporate boards and CEOs have this mind-set, too, a continuing phenomenon that emerged about 20 years ago. Most leaders see an executive in the ranks—even the best performers—as filling an assignment. When it's over—for strategic or financial reasons—so is the executive's tenure with the company.

On an intellectual level, most executives know that the assignment mentality rules. Even so, some allow that reality to recede in their minds; it's only human nature. Then they get fired or are laid off and, like clockwork, fall into one of three traps. The first is the "lost identity" trap. Executives in this group have, over months or years, allowed themselves to "become" their jobs. Unable to imagine their companies existing without them or themselves existing without their companies, they react to termination with rage, even vengeance. The second is the "lost family" trap, the province of executives who believe that their coworkers are more than that—dear friends, even a second family. Under these circumstances, termination becomes painful estrangement, with attendant feelings of betrayal and sorrow. Finally, there is the "lost ego" trap, in which executives silently retreat from the company without negotiating fair termination packages and

Idea in Brief

Even if you're a top-notch executive in the best of times, you can still lose your job. But can you lose it the *right* way?

For some executives, getting fired is cause for lashing out, sinking into depression, or silently retreating. But these responses make it difficult to generate new opportunities—and can destroy careers.

How can you avoid these termination traps and make the best of being fired? First, get rid of the "tenure mind-set"—

that falsely comforting sense that your organization will take care of you until you formally retire. Instead, adopt the "assignment mind-set"—seeing each job as a stepping-stone, a temporary project in your long-term career.

Then, take steps to control how you're fired—and how you respond. The payoff? You position yourself for excellent new opportunities *and* you make a great catch for your next employer. *You're* in control.

disappear into troughs of silent despair that make them reluctant to reach for the next opportunities.

We'll examine these traps, all of which can arise from being fired or laid off, in the following pages and then turn to a few strategies for making a dignified departure. But first, a few observations about the assignment mentality itself.

Which Mind-Set Do You Have?

The assignment model common in most companies today got its start in project-oriented industries—such as the arts, sports, agriculture, construction, and consulting. In these arenas, work comes and goes; individuals are contracted as needed; and work groups are continually assembled, altered, and dissolved. The assignment model presupposes the existence of "assignment

Idea in Practice

Termination Traps

Executives risk falling into these traps when losing a job:

Trap	Who's most susceptible	What happens
Lost identity	Founders, senior execs, long-time company leaders who've accumulated power and have "become" their jobs.	They fight back—lashing out against former employers and branding themselves as people no one wants to work with.
Lost family	Leaders in companies with high emotional intensity where people consider colleagues family.	They mourn—sinking into bitterness and depression, becoming unattractive candidates for future positions.
Lost ego	Introverts with top positions in areas requiring little outside interaction (e.g., accounting, engineering).	They fade away—neglecting to negotiate decent severance and refusing to network to generate new opportunities.

executives"—people hired for two to six years to guide and implement a company's strategy. Sometimes, a company itself may be on assignment, in the sense that its end is foreseeable: For example, a company faced with a short product life cycle, tough competition, or an unforgiving investment community may develop a corporate exit strategy. Such an exit strategy might be to increase shareholder value by 50% and then engineer an initial public offering or an acquisition by a larger competitor. Once this strategy is successful, a new group of senior managers replaces the outgoing one.

Assume You'll Be Fired—and Lay the Right Groundwork

How to manage the possibility of being fired? Accept the impermanence of your job, and take these systematic approaches to your next move:

- **Insert a termination clause in your employment contract**—Counterintuitive, yes, but it's your best hedge against a bitter exit. You're never as attractive as the day you sign your contract.

- **Schedule network phone calls**—Make networking a disciplined, regular part of doing business. Keep your web of professional contacts intact.

- **Raise your visibility**—Conduct your own public-relations campaign, keeping a strong industry profile. Serve on for-profit boards in and outside your industry. Volunteer for trade associations' externally oriented committees.

- **Watch for exit signs**—Getting fired should not come as a surprise. If your firm hustles people out the door, raise your own guard. If the company itself has an exit plan, find out how it affects your position. Consult with trusted, seasoned advisers who can alert you to potential changes.

- **Volunteer to be terminated**—if the firm's exit strategy includes you. This makes you the actor, rather than the one acted upon.

Although the assignment model is real, it is rarely discussed. A mythic belief lives alongside it in the minds of most employees. This is the "tenure mind-set"—the comforting sense that an organization willingly parts with valued employees only when they formally retire. It has long been dead in corporate America, although most companies won't openly admit it. After all, letting employees know that their jobs are finite would make them feel disposable and would hurt recruiting efforts. For this reason, most companies perpetuate the tenure myth, particularly in corporate literature. Annual reports and other accounts, filled with glowing language about career paths, continually work to persuade employees that companies take long-term views of their career development.

Most of the time, the assignment and tenure mindsets coexist peacefully. Externally hired CEOs truly understand that their jobs are pure assignments, because very specific termination and severance clauses are written into the employment contracts. For everyone else, the assignment nature of the job may not be clearly understood. Indeed, it's easy to ignore, even to deny. Moreover, senior executives tend to believe their own jobs are the most secure. And it isn't unusual for a founder, a CEO, or an executive promoted from within to be lulled into the tenure mind-set. When the company's exit strategy dictates a departure and sets in motion a collision between the two mind-sets, disillusionment can emerge and executives can fall into one of the three traps.

Caught in the Quagmire

When terminated suddenly, even the most widely admired and competent executives can be overcome by anger and grief. Saddled by these emotional responses, they may take actions they later regret. Let's take a closer look at these three traps.

The Lost Identity Trap
The people most susceptible to this trap are likely to have been with a company for some time; their jobs

may have been cut short due to a sudden change in course or a pressing financial crisis. Such people often include founders and senior executives who have achieved positions of power through promotion. In the day-to-day demands of doing their jobs, executives who fall into this trap have nurtured the strong sense that they are indispensable; they may have heard as much from investors or board members. Confronted with sudden job loss, they fall apart and often lash out against the former company—now rife with "enemies."

Consider Fred, a 31-year-old engineer who received his degree from MIT and then spent three years working for a large computer manufacturer. There, he developed a key technology that allowed companies to tap into their large databases via the Internet. After inventing the software, Fred decided to found a company with his own sweat equity; in time, he accepted funding from a venture capital firm with the understanding that he would be surrendering control of day-to-day operations to one of the venture partners. The partner said that Fred's continued presence was extremely important and that he hoped that Fred would consider assuming the role of chairman. Eager to finance his company, Fred agreed.

Eventually, the VC firm hired a permanent CEO, a 54-year-old man who had plenty of managerial experience but who lacked the technical skills that Fred so prized in himself. When he wanted to drive home a point, the CEO called Fred "son"; in response, Fred would mutter, "I already have a father." One day, the CEO and the VC met with Fred and fired him.

A few weeks later, Fred told us angrily, "I was kicked out of my own company." By then, Fred had done a lot of damage. In the days after his termination, he phoned each of the partners of the VC firm and accused them of betrayal. He refused to pass on his operational or engineering knowledge to anyone within the company. And when an industry analyst called to find out what had happened, Fred "secretly" confided his anger and frustration. Soon, word of Fred's unprofessional behavior circulated in both the large software industry and the small VC community. Eventually, Fred created a new start-up software company but, stamped as a person no one wanted to make deals with, was unable to secure further VC funding.

The Lost Family Trap

This trap is most prevalent among people working in fields like marketing or magazine publishing or within start-ups—all environments of high emotional intensity. Employees in such organizations can form tight-knit, emotional bonds, just as troops in combat do. These bonds can become so close that relationships with people outside work may seem dull.

Like the main character in the 1970s sitcom *The Mary Tyler Moore Show,* executives with such intense connections can make work the emotional center of their universe. Projecting familial roles upon colleagues, who become surrogate parents, siblings, aunts, or uncles, these executives suffer grief when, on termination, the "old gang" suddenly grows distant. But who can blame the coworkers? Suffering from survivor guilt and perhaps worrying about losing their own jobs, they're instinctively turning away from the person in pain. The coworkers, too, are in shock. Executives, however, caught emotionally in the lost family trap, can't see this. They feel as if friendships have been severed and they've been rejected. As a result, they sink into bitterness and depression.

Justine was the CEO of a consumer goods manufacturing company that had once dominated its marketplace. A 15-year veteran of her company, she was an energetic workaholic who felt alive only when she was at work. Justine loved her husband and children, but she found family life mundane compared with the adrenaline-pumping game of business. Over time, however, the company began losing market share. Although the members of the board liked Justine, they felt that the company needed to go in a completely new direction by taking its manufacturing offshore; Justine fought this idea because it meant shutting down facilities and laying off beloved workers. The board, impatient to reposition the company to take advantage of new opportunities, unanimously voted to let Justine go and replace her with a new CEO.

On an intellectual level, Justine understood that anyone can be fired. As head of the company, she had arranged enough terminations to know how the game is played. But upon being fired herself, Justine believed she had lost not only her job and income but also the de facto family of which she believed herself the matriarch. When she reached out to her former subordinates, whom she had protected and befriended, they did not have time to meet her for drinks or dinner and seemed uninterested in how she was faring. The truth was that her "family"was afraid to go near her for fear that merely associating with Justine would bring them to the board's attention.

Unable to hide her depression and bitterness, Justine became an unattractive candidate. Recruiters felt she had failed to manage her board properly and hadn't rebounded from an event that should have been predictable. Unable to find work, Justine purchased a franchise retail operation, whose employees became a replacement family—and from which she could never be fired.

The Lost Ego Trap

Executives who fall into the lost ego trap, in our observations, tend to be introverts. Such people work very effectively in areas of the company such as accounting and finance, R&D, manufacturing, or engineering, which don't demand high levels of socialization with outside constituencies. After being unexpectedly terminated, these executives tend to withdraw.

Consider Frank, a CFO for a retail company with $50 million in sales. As a child, Frank was shy and had few friends; although he loved playing the piano, he never enjoyed public performance. After majoring in math in college, Frank earned his CPA and followed a career in finance, eventually attaining the rank of CFO. He became the acting head of the company when the CEO, after a bitter divorce, escaped on his sailboat to cruise around the world and enjoy an extended vacation on a tropical island. Although Frank was competent enough to earn the owner's trust during this long sabbatical, he was not able to prevent a loss of market share when the economy hit tough times. The fall in the company's fortunes forced the CEO to cut short his holiday; upon his return, he fired Frank and resumed control of the business with an eye toward selling it.

Although he had been with the company for 12 years, Frank reacted to the news of his termination and scant severance without a complaint and quietly left, not wanting to make a fuss. It never occurred to him to consult an attorney skilled in severance negotiations for help in procuring a more generous termination package. Every book he read on job hunting recommended networking, but he just couldn't do it; he felt that the books were telling him to be someone he wasn't. Instead of reaching out to acquaintances or taking advantage of professional networks, he relied on third parties such as recruiters or on electronic job boards to find his next position; but these efforts produced few results.

Finally, an opportunity developed with a company 150 miles away from his home. Frank listened lackadaisically as the recruiter described the position. He was already conjuring the negative aspects of the deal. "I'll have to pull the kids out of school and away from all their friends," he thought. "My wife will have to quit the job she loves. We'll have to sell our wonderful home in an uncertain housing market." Frank told the recruiter he would think about it and hung up. But rather than balancing the imagined negatives with the job's prospective benefits—the stable and growing company, a generous relocation package, the excellent position with an equity stake—Frank focused only on the downsides, which combined into an excuse to turn down the prospect without further consideration. Eventually, he accepted a far less promising position within ten miles of his house.

Exiting with Aplomb

Executives can fall into these traps—of fighting back, mourning, or fading away—when they are reacting to sudden or unexpected events. Better, of course, to be prepared, and in a moment, we'll talk about how to do that. But first, here's a piece of tactical advice. When fired or being laid off, follow the old saying and count to 100 to cool down. That is, resist the impulse to say the first thing that comes into your mind. In fact, try not to say much of anything. Contact an attorney who negotiates severance packages for senior executives. Do not call colleagues, send e-mails, or speak to reporters. In the next 48 hours, people will be contacting you. Say nothing until the severance contract has been signed. It is also important that your spouse or partner stick to whatever "official story" is being developed about you and the company.

That's the short-term fix. Now let's explore longterm strategies for departing correctly. These strategies all involve a proactive—even calculated—approach to termination. They also require adoption of the assignment mind-set: by remaining conscious of the impermanence of their jobs, executives will avoid merely reacting and can adopt systematic approaches to the next move.

Rhonda exemplifies an executive who handled her termination the right way. As a child, she had been raised to believe the adage, "If you take care of the company, the company will take care of you." After completing her MBA, she moved to San Francisco and worked at a mid-sized software company. When she and all her colleagues lost their jobs during an acquisition, Rhonda reevaluated her tenure mind-set. The experience persuaded her that the familiar adage was no longer tenable, and she learned to treat successive opportunities as moves toward her career goal of becoming a successful CEO.

Eventually, a new e-commerce venture with a focus on distribution hired Rhonda as its CEO. A top-tier VC firm had proffered the first financing round of $3 million and also promised a second round of $7 million. Rhonda—now armed with assignment thinking—negotiated a one-year severance package at full pay as part of the employment contract. Soon afterward, she began growing the company, and the VC partner expressed satisfaction with her efforts. But instead of nursing illusions of permanence, Rhonda kept a weather eye out for signs of the company's approaching exit strategy. She likened her assignment to "parachuting onto a sailboat during a typhoon—I just landed with my hands on the tiller and went from there." Aware of the perilousness of e-commerce ventures, she cultivated her network for the day when she would need it. She served on two corporate boards, one a computer hardware company and the other a wireless communications company, and spent one night every two weeks staying in touch by phone with top business contacts. These were upbeat conversations; she never complained to other executives about her work.

In the spring of 2000, when the Internet bubble burst, the VC partner announced that not only would his firm not put in the $7 million but that it also wanted the whole operation shut down as soon as possible. Of course, Rhonda was angry at the partner for reneging on his promise. But she kept her negative feelings to herself; they passed soon enough, for she was well positioned for the next assignment. The venture capitalist was so impressed by Rhonda's behavior that he wrote a glowing letter of recommendation that complemented her own efforts to procure a new assignment as CEO of a new distribution company with ample financing and a strong market position.

The single most important key to Rhonda's success was her assignment mentality. Although the tenure mind-set had felt natural and comforting to her, she understood that even the most desirable job today is finite. She also understood that she was responsible for crafting her own exit strategy.

In managing current assignments and protecting options for the future, executives can follow Rhonda's example by adopting the following strategies. While not surprising or new, these tasks can be forgotten or postponed by executives too enmeshed in day-to-day work to take care of their careers. And these tactics can prove invaluable during termination.

Insert a Termination Clause in
Your Employment Contract

A new hire is never more attractive to the company than on the day before signing an employment contract; that's when you best control the terms of your employment. If you are newly hired or in the process of being promoted to a position that requires signing a new employment or confidentiality contract, it's possible to build your exit terms into the agreement. Like a prenuptial agreement that protects both sides if a marriage is dissolved, the insertion of such a clause at the time of hire feels completely counterintuitive. Nevertheless, it's your best hedge against a bitter exit. Hire a lawyer with experience in employment contract negotiation to insert clauses that will provide a satisfactory exit package in the event of termination.

Schedule Network Calls

Make networking a discipline, not a catch-as-catch-can activity. In an assignment-driven world, keeping one's network of professional acquaintances intact is time-consuming, but it's a critical cost of doing business. The importance of networking is obvious—which may be why managers, who sometimes put their own career needs on hold, rarely think of it. Unless network calls are explicitly scheduled and rigorously carried out, they can remain mere intentions. A biweekly calendar note reminds you to get in touch with the important people in your network—especially those with their own strong networks such as valued advisers to CEOs or partners within law, consulting, or accounting firms.

Raise Your Visibility—by Stealth

Most executives understand that if they conduct personal self-branding PR campaigns, their companies will automatically fire them; the only person with official sanction to "represent" the company is likely to be the CEO. On occasion, your company's public relations team may be able to provide you with speaking engagements or bylined articles in trade publications; but such opportunities can be rare.

That's where stealth comes in. You may not be able to talk to reporters, but you can certainly raise your visibility with other professionals. You can serve on for-profit boards, at least one of which should be in an industry other than your own. This is so important that we routinely suggest adding a clause requiring board service into an employment contract. In addition to garnering useful perspectives from peers in other arenas, serving on industry boards expands the network both within and beyond one's core business—making it possible to move into new companies and industries later on. You can also play a selective and strategic leadership role in a trade association. By volunteering for externally oriented committees—such as membership, marketing, legislative affairs, or programs—you'll be able to get in front of outside constituencies while retaining a strong industry profile.

Watch for Exit Signs

Being terminated should not come as a surprise, but it sometimes does. Some companies provide no warning to employees about to be terminated, for fear that advance notice may result in damage to the company—from sabotage of computer systems, for example. To be as prepared as possible, pay attention to your company's culture of termination (see the sidebar "Auf Wiedersehen: How to Fire Right"). Are people severed harshly and hustled out of the building, or is the door left open for a possible return? If the former, you may want to raise your guard and take some proactive steps. Likewise, watch for how the company itself is planning to exit, because your job depends on it. Examine the position and assignment changes within the company; do position descriptions or sets of responsibilities—including your own—imply an end? If yours does, it's entirely fair to ask whether your position will continue or how it will change once this particular work is complete. It's also helpful to cultivate a strong relationship with a founder or another trusted adviser who has "seen it all before"and who can help you stay aware of prospective changes. Remember—if you think you are about to be fired, you probably are. But if you are confused by signals being given to you, consider hiring an executive coach to help you sort them out (see the sidebar "Do You Need an Agent?").

Volunteer To Be Terminated

If the company's exit strategy appears to include you, consider volunteering to be terminated before it occurs. By initiating such a discussion, you become the actor rather than the one who is acted upon. Here's what happened when Joe, the CEO of a large firm, volunteered to be laid off as his company was acquired. The terms of

Auf Wiedersehen: How To Fire Right

EVERY INDUSTRY BOASTS COMPANIES with traditions of never rehiring people who leave, regardless of how well those employees perform. But given the growth of the assignment mind-set within corporations, the unprecedented ease of movement between companies, and the difficulty of attracting excellent employees, it no longer makes sense to slam the door behind departed workers who have been solid performers. After all, such employees do not simply vanish into the night. They go to professional meetings, where they can openly discuss their exit treatment with prospective recruits. Customers, strategic partners, distributors, or acquisition candidates may hire them. And once the noncompete clauses in their employment contracts expire, they might even decide to work for a competitor.

Many companies usher employees out the door with minimal termination packages, even sending them off under a cloud of humiliation. We call these "goodbye" terminations, because they deal in finality. In one goodbye termination, a CEO who had had a disagreement with the board was fired, although the company's press release claimed he had resigned. The chairman then issued an internal memo stating that the board had forced the CEO to resign. Employees saw the ashenfaced CEO clean out his desk and depart under the gaze of the HR vice president. Not surprisingly, morale within the company dropped precipitously, and several valued employees also quit.

A much better alternative to the goodbye termination is what we call the "auf Wiedersehen" (German for "until we see you again") termination. An auf Wiedersehen departure assumes that the company will meet the departing employee again in another context and thus conducts the termination as respectfully as possible. There are several advantages to this approach. First, by making an effort to preserve the employee's dignity and goodwill, the company decreases the chance of a backlash from the employee or of a sullied reputation for its act. Second, when there is a poor fit between an individual and a company, an auf Wiedersehen exit makes it easier for the employee to leave (or even quit) without causing trauma to the company or himself.

In addition, auf Wiedersehen terminations make it possible to re-recruit top-performing alumni. This makes excellent financial sense. According to the Corporate Leadership Council, it costs 176% of base salary to recruit and train a new IT professional and 241% of base salary to recruit and train a new middle manager. When alumni are re-recruited, costs drop to almost zero because companies don't have to pay search firms, interview candidates, train employees, or get them ramped up for productivity.

By keeping accurate performance records on past employees and staying in touch with excellent alumni, companies can also reduce the possibility of mis-hire, thus saving time and money. McKinsey, for example, sponsors alumni programs such as special breakfasts and on-line directories that allow former employees to keep in touch with the company and one another. Since alumni are also shareholders, the strong alumnishareholder base has helped attract and retain shareholders during economic downturns.

Using an auf Wiedersehen termination policy doesn't necessarily mean that companies must spend huge amounts on termination benefits; it merely requires that companies treat departing employees with the same respect when they leave as they received when they entered. Your pay policies should also be consistent. In comparisons with your competition, don't brag that you pay at the 75th percentile for new hires but at the 50th percentile for terminations. Pay policies and termination policies are two sides of one coin called "how people are treated."

Do You Need an Agent?

CONSIDER THE FOLLOWING SCENARIO: A recruiter calls you about a "fantastic" opportunity with another company, but you are too busy to give it serious attention. So you propose an alternative. "I want to give this opportunity the consideration it deserves," you say. "Given the demands of my current job, it would not be fair to my company to spend time with you. Let me give you the phone number of my agent. She understands what would be a good fit for me. My agent will do the initial screening. If the answer is yes, then we can talk in more detail. If it's no, I will be glad to refer you to others."

Tiger Woods benefits from having an agent, but a CEO? As far-fetched as it sounds, executive agents are part of a growing industry of coaches. The reason is simple. CEOs must focus their full attention on their current jobs, but in so doing, they forget to manage their careers. As a result, when assignments end, they can find themselves grasping at opportunities rather than making strategic moves.

A CEO agent helps clients with career strategy, presentation skills, image building, networking, and employment and salary negotiations. He or she also helps to screen job opportunities, even to manage money or save face in difficult situations. But is an executive agent necessary? As partners in an executive search, coaching, and outplacement firm, we can say, "Absolutely not." This kind of professional help makes little sense for extremely senior executives—CEOs like Jack Welch or Michael Dell, for example—who are very public symbols of their enterprises. Many groups within their corporations—such as the corporate public relations and investor relations departments, who keep the CEO's name in the public eye—already do some of the work of CEO agents.

Nor are CEOs who are between assignments good candidates for agents. A CEO agent manages an employed professional's long-term career; the first priority of any job candidate is to focus on securing the next assignment, and an outplacement firm would provide a sharper focus for such an individual. Outplacement services are usually provided to senior executives as part of termination packages and thus do not require personal expense.

Nevertheless, a CEO agent can play an important role, for example, in helping to negotiate the gray area of getting from one assignment to another. Eight months before the expiration of a CEO contract, a board may begin informal discussions about whether to renew the contract and may use a retained search firm to delicately explore alternatives. At the same time, a CEO's own agent can quietly explore new options. When the company and the CEO sit down to renegotiate the employment contract, both sides benefit from a clear sense of market conditions.

A CEO agent may do the legwork to manage an individual's reputation—that intangible asset that defines an executive's individual worth. One time-consuming aspect of reputation management is networking; focused on the demands of the job, an executive may lack the time to keep the network "warm." Consider Phil, a CEO with a network of 850 business contacts. He would reach out to his network only when he needed to find his next assignment; because he didn't otherwise maintain contact or contribute to committees or associations, he became known as a taker rather than as a giver. Phil commissioned a CEO agent to keep his network warm by sending quarterly personal letters, cards, and relevant articles to his contacts; Phil only signed the letters. As a result, the time he spent looking for a new position between assignments shrank from an average of six months to three.

A CEO agent can help, too, to ensure that an individual's public reputation remains strong. According to the public relations firm Burson-Marsteller, 45% of a company's reputation rests on that of its CEO. This percentage has increased almost 14% since 1997. Moreover, 95% of analysts who select stock use CEO reputation as a key decision point.

(Continued)

Do You Need an Agent? (continued)

A CEO agent sometimes acts as a career coach, a person familiar with your industry and company who can serve as a trusted, impartial sounding board and work behind the scenes to help you be more effective on the job. A coach is typically an experienced businessperson who, over the years, has developed a gift for navigating business dynamics and with whom the executive develops a close, one-on-one relationship. If, for example, an executive feels she's been given a cold shoulder by someone in the organization with whom she thought she had a good relationship, a coach can help her backtrack through communications to discern possible sources of contention. Or a coach might help an executive discover ways to sell an idea to various constituents within a company, such as strategizing on how to acquire ownership of other parts of a company while the executive maintains a focus on the core aspects of his or her job.

An agent can also supply an executive with a career management infrastructure—public relations professionals to generate a visibility program, administrative staff to keep a network warm, attorneys specializing in employment contract negotiation, financial planners, and outplacement consultants. An agent might even pair an executive with a theater director to assist with an important "performance."

As with any consulting arrangement, an executive who uses an agent should proceed with caution. Here's how.

Depend on Excellent References

CEO agents are difficult to find; good ones work strictly by referral. Other CEOs, or contacts in professions that use agents (sports, publishing, media), may be able to refer you to good ones. A few search firms also provide such services. Don't forget to seek help from associations such as the Young Presidents' Organization or Renaissance Executive Forums.

Ask Hard Questions

Before entering into a relationship with a CEO agent, hold an exploratory meeting or two during which you ask specific questions about how the agent would help manage your career for the long term. It's also important to have an open discussion about potential conflicts of interest, because the agent may know things about your company that you don't. If, for example, the agent works for a search firm that already has a relationship with your company, it's possible that the agent could be hired to find your successor. To circumvent problems, you and your agent should outline any potential conflicts of interest that either of you can imagine. And if, for any reason, the agent is not on your ethical wavelength, pass.

Understand the Arrangement

Don't hire a CEO agent for a onetime transaction. Like your CPA, financial planner, or attorney, your agent is a long-term valued adviser you expect to work with over many years. He or she must be available to you 24/7 to help you with specific work-related and career management issues; it's also wise to include your agent in occasional family discussions about plans and goals. Like professional recruiters and other personal consultants, a CEO agent is hired on retainer, typically charging 5% of the executive's cash compensation, with a $15,000 minimum yearly fee.

Set Realistic Goals

Work together with your agent to develop six-month and one-year game plans with pragmatic goals. You want to make discernable progress in expanding your visibility, but don't expect miracles. If you are an unknown CEO from a small firm, you probably won't be sitting on the board of a *Fortune* 500 company within three months. Before the annual contract comes up for renewal, meet with your agent to evaluate the year's accomplishments.

his existing contract allowed Joe to stay on for two years as president of the newly merged organization while the CEO of the acquiring company became chairman. But rather than waiting to be terminated after the contract expired, Joe approached the new chairman with a suggestion. Joe said that while he knew that the contract was a fair one, he fully appreciated that the acquiring company would want to run things differently. He offered to resign, provided that an excellent severance agreement could be developed. The chairman, delighted to be saved the trouble of firing Joe, was extraordinarily generous, and Joe's severance package allowed him to retire altogether.

We do not mean to suggest that executives become overly wary and move from job to job or from company to company too quickly; a lot of mobility is as damaging as a little. Rather, we posit that in most cases, a degree of self-interest in one's career—as understood in its broadest, lifespanning sense—is both healthy and necessary. Executives who hold on to the tenure myth may find it difficult to assume an assignment mentality, and understandably so. It's natural to want to believe that the company for which you work so hard cares about you. But allowing yourself to be lulled into a false sense of security sets you up for shock and disappointment when you are fired or laid off.

On the corporate level, terminations are among the most predictable crises in business. When you develop an assignment mind-set, your termination becomes predictable on a personal level, too. Then even an experience as negative as being fired can turn out to be strangely empowering. It's ironic, but true: When you assume control over the way you are fired, you can gain control over your career.

LAURENCE J. STYBEL and **MARYANNE PEABODY** are the founding partners of Stybel Peabody Lincolnshire, a Boston-based consulting firm.

Originally published in July 2001. Reprint R0107F

How to Protect Your Job in a Recession

by Janet Banks and Diane Coutu

IN A TROUBLED ECONOMY, job eliminations and hiring freezes seem almost routine, but when your own company's woes start to make headlines, it all hits home. Intellectually, you understand that downsizing isn't personal; it's just a law of commerce, but your heart sinks at the prospect of losing your position. While you know that passivity is a mistake, it's hard to be proactive when your boss's door is always closed, new projects are put on hold, and your direct reports look to you for reassurance. Don't panic. Even though layoff decisions may be beyond your control, there's plenty you can do.

That's what we've observed in numerous layoffs over the years and in research on how people respond to stressful work conditions. (Author Janet Banks oversaw a dozen downsizings as a vice president in human resources at Chase Manhattan Bank and a managing director at FleetBoston Financial. Author Diane Coutu studied resilience during her time as an affiliate scholar at the Boston Psychoanalytic Society and Institute.) We've seen that while luck plays an important role, survival is most often the result of staring reality in the face and making concrete plans to shape the future. Machiavellian as it may seem, holding on to your job when the economy softens is a matter of cool strategic planning. In our experience, however, even the savviest executives are ill-prepared to deal with job threats. Here's what you can do to keep your career moving and minimize the chances that you'll become a casualty.

Act Like a Survivor

A popular partner in the Brussels office of McKinsey & Company mentored hosts of junior consultants. When asked for advice on getting ahead, he always gave the same reply: "If you want to be a partner, start acting like one." The corollary of this advice is even more important: During a recession, you have to start acting like a survivor if you hope to escape the ax.

Studying the thinking of survivors reveals a surprising paradox. Though creating a plan to weather layoffs requires an almost pessimistic realism, the best thing you can do in a recession is lighten up. Keep your eye firmly on the eight ball, but act confident and cheerful. Research shows that being fun to be around really matters. Work by Tiziana Casciaro and Miguel Sousa Lobo, published in a June 2005 HBR article, "Competent Jerks, Lovable Fools, and the Formation of Social

Idea in Brief

Your company has a strategy for surviving hard times. But do you? In a troubled economy, layoffs can hit with frightening regularity. Sure, these decisions may be beyond your control. Yet you *can* take steps to protect your job, say Banks and Coutu.

Three practices can help you minimize the chances of becoming a casualty: 1) Act like a survivor by demonstrating confidence and staying focused on the future. 2) Give your boss hope by empathizing with him or her and inspiring your team to pull together. 3) Become a corporate citizen by taking part in meetings, outings, and new projects designed to support a reorganization.

Networks," shows that while everyone prefers working with a personable superstar to an incompetent jerk, when people need help getting a job done, they'll choose a congenial colleague over one who is more capable but less lovable. We're not suggesting that you morph into Jerry Seinfeld; being congenial and fun isn't about bringing down the house. Just don't be the guy who's always in a bad mood, reminding colleagues how vulnerable everyone is. Who wants to be in the trenches with him?

Of course, putting on a good face can be psychologically exhausting when rumors of downsizing spread. Change always stirs up fears of the unknown. Will you land another job? How will you pay the mortgage? Can you find affordable health insurance? Those are all valid concerns, but if you stay positive, you'll have more influence on how things play out.

Survivors are also forward looking. Studies of concentration camp victims show that people made it through by imagining a future for themselves. The power of

BANKS AND COUTU

Idea in Practice

Banks and Coutu recommend three strategies for recession-proofing your job.

Act Like a Survivor

If you want to *be* a layoff survivor, it helps to act like one:

- **Demonstrate confidence and cheerfulness.** When people need help getting jobs done, they'll choose a congenial colleague over an unlikeable one. No one wants to be in the trenches with someone who's always gloomy.

- **Keep your eye on the future.** There's no better way to look forward than to sharpen your focus on customers. Without them, no one will have a job in the future. Make anticipating customers' needs your top

priority. And show how your work is relevant to meeting those needs.

- **Wear multiple hats.** To keep expenses in check, look for opportunities to play more than one role and leverage your diverse experiences. For instance, a marketing manager who had previously taught school volunteered to take on sales training responsibilities.

Give Your Boss Hope

The better your relationship with your manager, the less likely it is that you'll be cut. Strengthen that bond through these practices:

- **Empathize.** Most leaders find layoffs agonizing. By empathizing with your

focusing on the times ahead is evident even among people suffering the blows of everyday life. As Freud wrote in "Mourning and Melancholia," a critical difference between ordinary grief and acute depression is that mourners can successfully anticipate a life where there will once again be joy and meaning.

In your job, there's no better way to look forward than to stay focused on customers, for without them no one will have a job in the future. Anticipating the needs of your customers, both external and internal, should manager, you deepen your bond. You also demonstrate a maturity that's invaluable—because it models good behavior for others.

- **Unite and inspire your colleagues.** This ability can prove crucial during the worst of times.

  Example: At an international financial services company that had endured a 20% staff reduction, morale had plummeted. Isaac, a learning and development VP, assembled a team of volunteers who created a live radio show that engaged even cynical employees. It included a soap opera that kept staff laughing and waiting for the next episode. And it gave executives a platform to share key information, such as the company's performance and structural changes. Morale improved, and Isaac eventually became head of management and leadership development.

Become a Corporate Citizen

Eighty percent of success is showing up. To become a corporate citizen:

- Attend all voluntary and informal meetings and corporate outings.

- Get out of your office and walk the floor to see how people are doing.

- Get on board with new initiatives; for example, by volunteering to lead a newly formed team crucial to your company's recovery strategy.

be your top priority. Prove your value to the firm by showing your relevance to the work at hand, which may have shifted since the economy softened. Your job is less likely to be eliminated if customers find that your contribution is indispensable.

Being ambidextrous will increase your chances of survival as well. In one company we know of, senior staff members were often expected to play more than one role to keep expenses in check. When the organization's new chief operating officer decided he needed a chief of staff, he chose a person who continued to manage a human resources team, thereby eliminating the need for additional head count. Reorganizations and consolidations involve great change, so they demand versatile executives. If you're not already wearing multiple hats, start imagining how you can support your company by leveraging experience your boss may know nothing about. A marketing manager who taught school before moving into industry might volunteer to take on sales and service training responsibilities, for example. A recession can offer you plenty of opportunities to display your capabilities. Layoffs typically occur at all levels of an organization and can create vacuums above and below you.

Finally, survivors are willing to swallow a little pride. Take the case of Anne, a manager at a large New England insurance company. (We've changed her name, as well as those of the other individuals cited in this article.) During a reorganization, Anne found herself vying for a position with a colleague who had far less industry experience than she did. When she learned that she and her department would be folded under this colleague's department, Anne realized that she had one choice if she wanted to keep her job—use her significant influence to support her new manager. So she publicly threw herself behind the colleague. In turn, he gave her the respect and the loyalty she felt she deserved. Anne's attitude demonstrated commitment to the company—something that was noticed by the management. A year later Anne got new responsibilities that led to a prestigious board appointment.

Give Your Leaders Hope

It's important to recognize that times of uncertainty are also tough for leaders. They don't enjoy having to lay off their people; most find that task agonizing. It can be stressful and time-consuming for them to sort through the various change mandates they've been given and then decide what to do. Obviously, this isn't the time to push for a promotion or to argue for a new job title. Instead, try to help the leader defend your department. If the boss is working on a restructuring plan and asks for ideas, offer some realistic solutions. Don't fight change; energize your colleagues around it.

It may sound like what Karl Marx called *false consciousness*—thinking that disempowers you because it is not in your best interest—to empathize with your boss when he or she is considering cutting your job. However, there's science to support the idea that showing empathy for people more powerful than you can be worthwhile. For example, recent mother-infant research shows that the more an infant smiles and interacts with the environment, the more active the caretaker becomes in the infant's development and survival. Although the mother-infant research has not, to our knowledge, been replicated in the workplace, psychologists have shown that so-called attachment behavior—emotional bonding—can be learned, just as emotional intelligence skills can be honed. That's good news. The better your relationship with your manager, the less likely you are to be cut, all things being equal. Your ability to empathize can demonstrate a maturity that is invaluable to the company, not least because it models good behavior for others.

The ability to unite and inspire colleagues goes a long way in the best of times; in the worst it's crucial. This was true at an international financial services company that had endured a staff reduction of 20%. In the face of low morale, the head of human resources asked Isaac, a learning and development VP, to help revive people's spirits, improve communications, and stir up some fun. Isaac quickly pulled together a small team of volunteers and created a live radio show that engaged even the most cynical members of the organization. It included a soap opera that kept staff at all levels laughing and waiting for the next episode. The show gave executives a unique platform to share information such as quarterly financial results and changes in the organization's structure. It did so much to improve morale that as a result Isaac landed the job he wanted—head of management and leadership development for the company.

Become a Corporate Citizen

Remember Woody Allen's remark that 80% of success is showing up? That is especially useful advice in a downturn. Start going to all those voluntary and informal meetings you used to skip. Be visible. Get out of your office and walk the floor to see how folks are doing. Take part in company outings; if the firm is gathering for the annual golf tournament and you can't tell a wood from an iron, then go along just for fun. In tough times, leaders look for employees who are enthusiastic participants. It's not the score that counts.

Corporate citizens are quick to get on board. Consider Linda, a VP in operations, who worked in a large company that needed to cut costs. Management came up with the idea of shared service centers to avoid duplication of effort in staff functions in areas such as compensation, management training, and strategic planning. The decision was universally unpopular. Service center jobs had none of the cachet of working in small business units, where customized solutions could be developed. Headquarters staff objected to losing the elite status they'd enjoyed as corporate experts. When service center jobs were posted, many high-profile people refused to put their names forward, misjudging their own importance and hoping management would relent. But Linda saw the opportunity and applied for a service center job. The new position gave her immense visibility and was an immediate promotion. Meanwhile, many of the resisters found themselves standing without a chair when the music stopped. In contrast, Linda kept her career on track; six years later she reported directly to the president of the company.

Of course, changing your behavior or personality to survive may rub against your need for authenticity, and you may decide that it's time to move on. In that case, you can be both true to yourself and the ultimate corporate citizen by volunteering to leave the organization. Despite what the policy may be, companies will cut deals. Deals are even welcomed. It's much less painful for managers if they can help someone out the door

Preparing for the Worst: You May Still Need a Plan B

FOLLOWING THE BEST ADVICE is no guarantee that you won't get laid off. That's why you need a plan for handling a job loss.

The first key to moving on successfully is self-awareness. You'll have better luck finding a new job if you know what you're good at and what you'd really like to do, so it's wise to invest mental energy now in figuring those things out. If you have results from a Myers-Briggs test or a 360-degree assessment, revisit them to understand your strengths and weaknesses. Read self-help books to inspire your thinking, or perhaps even hire an executive coach. (Just make sure to get references and agree on fees before you start with any coach.)

Don't wait till you get laid off to update your résumé. Revise it now, so that you'll have it ready when you start approaching headhunters, former bosses and colleagues, and industry contacts for job referrals and advice. It's a good idea to begin networking with those folks now, in fact, but don't stop there. Reach out to the neighbor who's the CFO of a successful company, and dig out the old business cards from your drawer and add those names to the list of those you'll call.

Finally, think creatively about your future. Perhaps you want to go back to school, start your own business, join a smaller firm, or become a minister. That may require some downsizing of your own, but as Ellen, a consultant, told us: "Now that the kids are grown, my husband looks at the house and says it's too big for the two of us. I'm willing to scale back. Both of us want to do different things." Who knows, maybe plan B will actually be more attractive than plan A.

---

who wants to leave rather than give bad news to someone who depends on the job. If you're a couple of years away from retirement eligibility and want to go, ask the company if it would be willing to bridge the time. Float a few balloons, but don't get greedy. Keep in mind that even if you choose to go, you may need to get another job and you'll want good references and referrals. If you've exited gracefully, odds are, your boss and others will do whatever they can to help you land on your feet.

———————————

Many forces are beyond your control in a recession, but if you direct your energy toward developing a strategy, you'll have a better chance of riding out the storm. You have to be extremely competent to make it through, but your attitude, your willingness to help the boss get the job done, and your contribution as a corporate citizen have a big impact on whether you are asked to stick around. The economy will bounce back; your job is to make sure that you do, too.

JANET BANKS has been an executive coach, an organizational consultant, and an executive search consultant. She does small group facilitation work for nonprofits. **DIANE COUTU** has been a communications specialist at McKinsey & Company, an affiliate scholar at the Boston Psychoanalytic Society and Institute, and a senior editor at HBR.

Originally published in September 2008. Reprint R0809J

How Leaders Create and Use Networks

by Herminia Ibarra and Mark Hunter

WHEN HENRIK BALMER BECAME the production manager and a board member of a newly bought-out cosmetics firm, improving his network was the last thing on his mind. The main problem he faced was time: Where would he find the hours to guide his team through a major upgrade of the production process and then think about strategic issues like expanding the business? The only way he could carve out time and still get home to his family at a decent hour was to lock himself—literally—in his office. Meanwhile, there were day-to-day issues to resolve, like a recurring conflict with his sales director over custom orders that compromised production efficiency. Networking, which Henrik defined as the unpleasant task of trading favors with strangers, was a luxury he could not afford. But when a new acquisition was presented at a board meeting without his input, he abruptly realized he was out of the loop—not just inside the company, but outside, too—at a moment when his future in the company was at stake.

Henrik's case is not unusual. Over the past two years, we have been following a cohort of 30 managers making their way through what we call the leadership transition, an inflection point in their careers that challenges them to rethink both themselves and their roles. In the process, we've found that networking—creating a fabric of personal contacts who will provide support, feedback, insight, resources, and information—is simultaneously one of the most self-evident and one of the most dreaded developmental challenges that aspiring leaders must address.

Their discomfort is understandable. Typically, managers rise through the ranks by dint of a strong command of the technical elements of their jobs and a nose-to-the-grindstone focus on accomplishing their teams' objectives. When challenged to move beyond their functional specialties and address strategic issues facing the overall business, many managers do not immediately grasp that this will involve relational—not analytical—tasks. Nor do they easily understand that exchanges and interactions with a diverse array of current and potential stakeholders are not distractions from their "real work" but are actually at the heart of their new leadership roles.

Like Henrik (whose identity we've disguised, along with all the other managers we describe here), a majority of the managers we work with say that they find networking insincere or manipulative—at best, an elegant way of using people. Not surprisingly, for every manager

Idea in Brief

What separates successful leaders from the rest of the pack? Networking: creating a tissue of personal contacts to provide the support, feedback, and resources needed to get things done.

Yet many leaders avoid networking. Some think they don't have time for it. Others disdain it as manipulative.

To succeed as a leader, Ibarra and Hunter recommend building three types of networks:

- **Operational**—people you need to accomplish your assigned, routine tasks.

- **Personal**—kindred spirits outside your organization who can help you with personal advancement.

- **Strategic**—people outside your control who will enable you to reach key organizational objectives.

You need all three types of networks. But to really succeed, you must master strategic networking—by interacting regularly with people who can open your eyes to new business opportunities and help you capitalize on them. Build your strategic network, and burnish your own—and your company's—performance.

who instinctively constructs and maintains a useful network, we see several who struggle to overcome this innate resistance. Yet the alternative to networking is to fail—either in reaching for a leadership position or in succeeding at it.

Watching our emerging leaders approach this daunting task, we discovered that three distinct but interdependent forms of networking—*operational, personal,* and *strategic*—played a vital role in their transitions. The first helped them manage current internal responsibilities, the second boosted their personal development, and the third opened their eyes to new business directions and the stakeholders they would need to

Idea in Practice

The most effective leaders understand the differences among the three types of networks and how to build them.

	Operational network	Personal network	Strategic network
Network's purpose	Getting work done efficiently	Develop professional skills through coaching and mentoring; exchange important referrals and needed outside information.	Figure out future priorities and challenges; get stakeholder support for them.
How to find network members	Identify individuals who can block or support a project.	Participate in professional associations, alumni groups, clubs, and personal-interest communities.	Identify lateral and vertical relationships with other functional and business-unit managers—people outside your immediate control—who can help you determine how your role and contribution fit into the overall picture.

enlist. While our managers differed in how well they pursued operational and personal networking, we discovered that almost all of them underutilized strategic networking. In this article, we describe key features of each networking form (summarized in the exhibit "The three forms of networking") and, using our managers' experiences, explain how a three-pronged networking strategy can become part and parcel of a new leader's development plan.

Leveraging Your Networks

Networking takes work. To lessen the pain and increase the gain:

- **Mind your mind-set.** Accept that networking is one of the most important requirements of a leadership role. To overcome any qualms about it, identify a person you respect who networks effectively and ethically. Observe how he or she uses networks to accomplish goals.

- **Reallocate your time.** Master the art of delegation, to liberate time you can then spend on cultivating networks.

- **Establish connections.** Create reasons for interacting with people outside your function or organization; for instance, by taking advantage of social interests to set the stage for addressing strategic concerns.

  Example: An investment banker invited key clients to the theatre (a passion of hers) several times a year. Through these events, she developed her own business *and* learned things about her clients' companies that generated business and ideas for other divisions in her firm.

- **Give and take continually.** Don't wait until you really need something badly to ask for a favor from a network member. Instead, take every opportunity to give to—and receive from—people in your networks, whether you need help or not.

Operational Networking

All managers need to build good working relationships with the people who can help them do their jobs. The number and breadth of people involved can be impressive—such operational networks include not only direct reports and superiors but also peers within an operational unit, other internal players with the power to block or support a project, and key outsiders such as

The three forms of networking

Managers who think they are adept at networking are often operating only at an operational or personal level. Effective leaders learn to employ networks for strategic purposes.

	Operational	Personal	Strategic
Purpose	Getting work done efficiently; maintaining the capacities and functions required of the group.	Enhancing personal and professional development; providing referrals to useful information and contacts.	Figuring out future priorities and challenges; getting stakeholder support for them.
Location and temporal orientation	Contacts are mostly internal and oriented toward current demands.	Contacts are mostly external and oriented toward current interests and future potential interests.	Contacts are internal and external and oriented toward the future.
Players and recruitment	Key contacts are relatively nondiscretionary; they are prescribed mostly by the task and organizational structure, so it is very clear who is relevant.	Key contacts are mostly discretionary; it is not always clear who is relevant.	Key contacts follow from the strategic context and the organizational environment, but specific membership is discretionary; it is not always clear who is relevant.
Network attributes and key behaviors	Depth: building strong working relationships.	Breadth: reaching out to contacts who can make referrals.	Leverage: creating inside-outside links.

suppliers, distributors, and customers. The purpose of this type of networking is to ensure coordination and co-operation among people who have to know and trust one another in order to accomplish their immediate tasks. That isn't always easy, but it is relatively straightforward, because the task provides focus and a clear criterion for membership in the network: Either you're necessary to the job and helping to get it done, or you're not.

Although operational networking was the form that came most naturally to the managers we studied, nearly every one had important blind spots regarding people and groups they depended on to make things happen. In one case, Alistair, an accounting manager who worked in an entrepreneurial firm with several hundred employees, was suddenly promoted by the company's founder to financial director and given a seat on the board. He was both the youngest and the least-experienced board member, and his instinctive response to these new responsibilities was to reestab-lish his functional credentials. Acting on a hint from the founder that the company might go public, Alistair undertook a reorganization of the accounting depart-ment that would enable the books to withstand close scrutiny. Alistair succeeded brilliantly in upgrading his team's capabilities, but he missed the fact that only a minority of the seven-person board shared the founder's ambition. A year into Alistair's tenure, discus-sion about whether to take the company public polar-ized the board, and he discovered that all that time cleaning up the books might have been better spent sounding out his codirectors.

One of the problems with an exclusive reliance on operational networks is that they are usually geared toward meeting objectives as assigned, not toward asking the strategic question, "What *should* we be doing?" By the same token, managers do not exercise as much personal choice in assembling operational relationships as they do in weaving personal and strategic networks, because to a large extent the right relationships are prescribed by the job and organizational structure. Thus, most operational networking occurs within an organization, and ties are determined in large part by routine, short-term demands. Relationships formed with outsiders, such as board members, customers, and regulators, are directly task-related and tend to be bounded and constrained by demands determined at a higher level. Of course, an individual manager can choose to deepen and develop the ties to different extents, and all managers exercise discretion over who gets priority attention. It's the quality of relationships—the rapport and mutual trust—that gives an operational network its power. Nonetheless, the substantial constraints on network membership mean these connections are unlikely to deliver value to managers beyond assistance with the task at hand.

The typical manager in our group was more concerned with sustaining cooperation within the existing network than with building relationships to face non-routine or unforeseen challenges. But as a manager moves into a leadership role, his or her network must reorient itself externally and toward the future.

Personal Networking

We observed that once aspiring leaders like Alistair awaken to the dangers of an excessively internal focus, they begin to seek kindred spirits outside their organizations. Simultaneously, they become aware of the limitations of their social skills, such as a lack of knowledge about professional domains beyond their own, which makes it difficult for them to find common ground with people outside their usual circles. Through professional associations, alumni groups, clubs, and personal interest communities, managers gain new perspectives that allow them to advance in their careers. This is what we mean by personal networking.

Many of the managers we study question why they should spend precious time on an activity so indirectly related to the work at hand. Why widen one's circle of casual acquaintances when there isn't time even for urgent tasks? The answer is that these contacts provide important referrals, information, and, often, developmental support such as coaching and mentoring. A newly appointed factory director, for example, faced with a turnaround-or-close-down situation that was paralyzing his staff, joined a business organization— and through it met a lawyer who became his counsel in the turnaround. Buoyed by his success, he networked within his company's headquarters in search of someone who had dealt with a similar crisis. Eventually, he found two mentors.

A personal network can also be a safe space for personal development and as such can provide a foundation for strategic networking. The experience of Timothy, a principal in a midsize software company, is a good example. Like his father, Timothy stuttered. When he had the opportunity to prepare for meetings, his stutter was not an issue, but spontaneous encounters inside and outside the company were dreadfully painful. To solve this problem, he began accepting at least two invitations per week to the social gatherings he had assiduously ignored before. Before each event, he asked who else had been invited and did background research on the other guests so that he could initiate conversations. The hardest part, he said, was "getting through the door." Once inside, his interest in the conversations helped him forget himself and master his stutter. As his stutter diminished, he also applied himself to networking across his company, whereas previously he had taken refuge in his technical expertise. Like Timothy, several of our emerging leaders successfully used personal networking as a relatively safe way to expose problems and seek insight into solutions—safe, that is, compared with strategic networking, in which the stakes are far higher.

Personal networks are largely external, made up of discretionary links to people with whom we have something in common. As a result, what makes a personal network powerful is its referral potential. According to the famous six degrees of separation principle, our personal contacts are valuable to the extent that they help us reach, in as few connections as possible, the far-off person who has the information we need.

In watching managers struggle to widen their professional relationships in ways that feel both natural and legitimate to them, we repeatedly saw them shift their time and energy from operational to personal networking. For people who have rarely looked outside their organizations, this is an important first step, one that fosters a deeper understanding of themselves and the environments in which they move. Ultimately, however, personal networking alone won't propel managers through the leadership transition. Aspiring leaders may find people who awaken new interests but fail to become comfortable with the power players at the level above them. Or they may achieve new influence within a professional community but fail to harness those ties in the service of organizational goals. That's why managers who know they need to develop their networking skills, and make a real effort to do so, nonetheless may end up feeling like they have wasted their time and energy. As we'll see, personal networking will not help a manager through the leadership transition unless he or she learns how to bring those connections to bear on organizational strategy.

Strategic Networking

When managers begin the delicate transition from functional manager to business leader, they must start to concern themselves with broad strategic issues. Lateral and vertical relationships with other functional and business unit managers—all people outside their immediate control—become a lifeline for figuring out how their own contributions fit into the big picture. Thus strategic networking plugs the aspiring leader into a set

From Functional Manager to Business Leader: How Companies Can Help

EXECUTIVES WHO OVERSEE MANAGEMENT development know how to spot critical inflection points: the moments when highly successful people must change their perspective on what is important and, accordingly, how they spend their time. Many organizations still promote people on the basis of their performance in roles whose requirements differ dramatically from those of leadership roles. And many new leaders feel that they are going it alone, without coaching or guidance. By being sensitive to the fact that most strong technical or functional managers lack the capabilities required to build strategic networks that advance their personal and professional goals, human resources and learning professionals can take steps to help in this important area.

For example, Genesis Park, an innovative in-house leadership development program at PricewaterhouseCoopers, focuses explicitly on building networks. The five-month program, during which participants are released from their client responsibilities, includes business case development, strategic projects, team building, change management projects, and in-depth discussions with business leaders from inside and outside the company. The young leaders who participate end up with a strong internal-external nexus of ties to support them as their careers evolve.

of relationships and information sources that collectively embody the power to achieve personal and organizational goals.

Operating beside players with diverse affiliations, backgrounds, objectives, and incentives requires a manager to formulate business rather than functional objectives, and to work through the coalitions and networks needed to sell ideas and compete for resources. Consider

Companies that recognize the importance of leadership networking can also do a lot to help people overcome their innate discomfort by creating natural ways for them to extend their networks. When Nissan CEO Carlos Ghosn sought to break down crippling internal barriers at the company, he created cross-functional teams of middle managers from diverse units and charged them with proposing solutions to problems ranging from supply costs to product design. Nissan subsequently institutionalized the teams, not just as a way to solve problems but also to encourage lateral networks. Rather than avoid the extra work, aspiring leaders ask for these assignments.

Most professional development is based on the notion that successful people acquire new role-appropriate skills as they move up the hierarchy. But making the transition from manager to leader requires subtraction as well as addition: To make room for new competencies, managers must rely less on their older, well-honed skills. To do so, they must change their perspective on how to add value and what to contribute. Eventually, they must also transform how they think and who they are. Companies that help their top talent reinvent themselves will better prepare them for a successful leadership transition.

Sophie, a manager who, after rising steadily through the ranks in logistics and distribution, was stupefied to learn that the CEO was considering a radical reorganization of her function that would strip her of some responsibilities. Rewarded to date for incremental annual improvements, she had failed to notice shifting priorities in the wider market and the resulting internal shuffle for resources and power at the higher levels of her company.

Although she had built a loyal, high-performing team, she had few relationships outside her group to help her anticipate the new imperatives, let alone give her ideas about how to respond. After she argued that distribution issues were her purview, and failed to be persuasive, she hired consultants to help her prepare a counterproposal. But Sophie's boss simply concluded that she lacked a broad, longer-term business perspective. Frustrated, Sophie contemplated leaving the company. Only after some patient coaching from a senior manager did she understand that she had to get out of her unit and start talking to opinion leaders inside and outside the company to form a sellable plan for the future.

What differentiates a leader from a manager, research tells us, is the ability to figure out where to go and to enlist the people and groups necessary to get there. Recruiting stakeholders, lining up allies and sympathizers, diagnosing the political landscape, and brokering conversations among unconnected parties are all part of a leader's job. As they step up to the leadership transition, some managers accept their growing dependence on others and seek to transform it into mutual influence. Others dismiss such work as "political" and, as a result, undermine their ability to advance their goals.

Several of the participants in our sample chose the latter approach, justifying their choice as a matter of personal values and integrity. In one case, Jody, who managed a department in a large company under what she described as "dysfunctional" leadership, refused even to try to activate her extensive network within the firm when internal adversaries took over key functions of her unit. When we asked her why she didn't seek help from anyone in the organization to stop this coup, she replied that she refused to play "stupid political games. ... You can only do what you think is the ethical and right thing from your perspective." Stupid or not, those games cost her the respect and support of her direct reports and coworkers, who hesitated to follow someone they perceived as unwilling to defend herself. Eventually she had no choice but to leave.

The key to a good strategic network is leverage: the ability to marshal information, support, and resources from one sector of a network to achieve results in another. Strategic networkers use indirect influence, convincing one person in the network to get someone else, who is not in the network, to take a needed action. Moreover, strategic networkers don't just influence their relational environment; they shape it in their own image by moving and hiring subordinates, changing suppliers and sources of financing, lobbying to place allies in peer positions, and even restructuring their boards to create networks favorable to their business goals. Jody abjured such tactics, but her adversaries did not.

Strategic networking can be difficult for emerging leaders because it absorbs a significant amount of the time and energy that managers usually devote to meeting their many operational demands. This is one reason why many managers drop their strategic networking precisely when they need it most: when their units are in trouble and only outside support can rescue them.

The trick is not to hide in the operational network but to develop it into a more strategic one.

One manager we studied, for example, used lateral and functional contacts throughout his firm to resolve tensions with his boss that resulted from substantial differences in style and strategic approaches between the two. Tied down in operational chores at a distant location, the manager had lost contact with headquarters. He resolved the situation by simultaneously obliging his direct reports to take on more of the local management effort and sending messages through his network that would help bring him back into the loop with the boss.

Operational, personal, and strategic networks are not mutually exclusive. One manager we studied used his personal passion, hunting, to meet people from professions as diverse as stonemasonry and household moving. Almost none of these hunting friends had anything to do with his work in the consumer electronics industry, yet they all had to deal with one of his own daily concerns: customer relations. Hearing about their problems and techniques allowed him to view his own from a different perspective and helped him define principles that he could test in his work. Ultimately, what began as a personal network of hunting partners became operationally and strategically valuable to this manager. The key was his ability to build inside-outside links for maximum leverage. But we've seen others who avoided networking, or failed at it, because they let interpersonal chemistry, not strategic needs, determine which relationships they cultivated.

Just Do It

The word "work" is part of networking, and it is not easy work, because it involves reaching outside the borders of a manager's comfort zone. How, then, can managers lessen the pain and increase the gain? The trick is to leverage the elements from each domain of networking into the others—to seek out personal contacts who can be objective, strategic counselors, for example, or to transform colleagues in adjacent functions into a constituency. Above all, many managers will need to change their attitudes about the legitimacy and necessity of networking.

Mind Your Mind-Set

In our ongoing discussions with managers learning to improve their networking skills, we often hear, "That's all well and good, but I already have a day job." Others, like Jody, consider working through networks a way to rely on "whom you know" rather than "what you know"—a hypocritical, even unethical way to get things done. Whatever the reason, when aspiring leaders do not believe that networking is one of the most important requirements of their new jobs, they will not allocate enough time and effort to see it pay off.

The best solution we've seen to this trap is a good role model. Many times, what appears to be unpalatable or unproductive behavior takes on a new light when a person you respect does it well and ethically. For example, Gabriel Chenard, general manager for Europe of a group of consumer product brands, learned from the previous general manager how to take advantage of branch visits to solidify his relationships with employees and customers. Every flight and car trip became a venue for catching up and building relationships with the people who were accompanying him. Watching how much his boss got done on what would otherwise be downtime, Gabriel adopted the practice as a crucial part of his own management style. Networking effectively and ethically, like any other tacit skill, is a matter of judgment and intuition. We learn by observing and getting feedback from those for whom it's second nature.

Work from the Outside In

One of the most daunting aspects of strategic networking is that there often seems to be no natural "excuse" for making contact with a more senior person outside one's function or business unit. It's difficult to build a relationship with anyone, let alone a senior executive, without a reason for interacting, like a common task or a shared purpose.

Some successful managers find common ground from the outside in—by, for instance, transposing a personal interest into the strategic domain. Linda Henderson is a good example. An investment banker responsible for a group of media industry clients, she always wondered how to connect to some of her senior colleagues who served other industries. She resolved to make time for an extracurricular passion—the theater—in a way that would enhance her business development activities. Four times a year, her secretary booked a buffet dinner at a downtown hotel and reserved a block of theater tickets.

Key clients were invited. Through these events, Linda not only developed her own business but also learned about her clients' companies in a way that generated ideas for other parts of her firm, thus enabling her to engage with colleagues.

Other managers build outside-inside connections by using their functional interests or expertise. For example, communities of practice exist (or can easily be created on the Internet) in almost every area of business from brand management to Six Sigma to global strategy. Savvy managers reach out to kindred spirits outside their organizations to contribute and multiply their knowledge; the information they glean, in more cases than not, becomes the "hook" for making internal connections.

Re-Allocate Your Time

If an aspiring leader has not yet mastered the art of delegation, he or she will find many reasons not to spend time networking. Participating in formal and informal meetings with people in other units takes time away from functional responsibilities and internal team affairs. Between the obvious payoff of a task accomplished and the ambiguous, often delayed rewards of networking, naive managers repeatedly choose the former. The less they practice networking, the less efficient at it they become, and the vicious cycle continues.

Henrik, the production manager and board member we described earlier, for example, did what he needed to do in order to prepare for board meetings but did not associate with fellow board members outside those formal events. As a result, he was frequently surprised when other board members raised issues at the heart of his role. In contrast, effective business leaders spend a lot of time every day gathering the information they need to meet their goals, relying on informal discussions with a lot of people who are not necessarily in charge of an issue or task. They network in order to obtain information continually, not just at formal meetings.

Ask and You Shall Receive

Many managers equate having a good network with having a large database of contacts, or attending high-profile professional conferences and events. In fact, we've seen people kick off a networking initiative by improving their record keeping or adopting a network management tool. But they falter at the next step—picking up the phone. Instead, they wait until they need something *badly*. The best networkers do exactly the opposite: They take every opportunity to give to, and receive from, the network, whether they need help or not.

A network lives and thrives only when it is used. A good way to begin is to make a simple request or take the initiative to connect two people who would benefit from meeting each other. Doing something—anything—gets the ball rolling and builds confidence that one does, in fact, have something to contribute.

Stick to it. It takes a while to reap the benefits of networking. We have seen many managers resolve to put networking at the top of their agendas, only to be derailed by the first crisis that comes along. One example is Harris Roberts, a regulatory affairs expert who realized he needed a broader network to achieve his goal of becoming a business unit manager. To force himself into what felt like an "unnatural act," Harris volunteered to be the liaison for his business school cohort's alumni network. But six months later, when a major new-drug approval process overwhelmed his calendar, Harris dropped all outside activities. Two years later, he found himself out of touch and still a functional manager. He failed to recognize that by not taking the time to attend industry conferences or compare notes with his peers, he was missing out on the strategic perspective and information that would make him a more attractive candidate for promotion.

Building a leadership network is less a matter of skill than of will. When first efforts do not bring quick rewards, some may simply conclude that networking isn't among their talents. But networking is not a talent; nor does it require a gregarious, extroverted personality. It is a skill, one that takes practice. We have seen over and over again that people who work at networking can learn not only how to do it well but also how to enjoy it. And they tend to be more successful in their careers than those who fail to leverage external ties or insist on defining their jobs narrowly.

Making a successful leadership transition requires a shift from the confines of a clearly defined operational network. Aspiring leaders must learn to build and use strategic networks that cross organizational and functional boundaries, and then link them up in novel and innovative ways. It is a challenge to make the leap from a lifetime of functional contributions and hands-on control to the ambiguous process of building and working through networks. Leaders must find new ways of defining themselves and develop new relationships to anchor and feed their emerging personas. They must also accept that networking is one of the most important requirements of their new leadership roles and continue to allocate enough time and effort to see it pay off.

HERMINIA IBARRA is a professor of organizational behavior at Insead in France and the author of *Working Identity: Unconventional Strategies for Reinventing Your Career* (Harvard Business Review Press, 2003). **MARK HUNTER** is an investigative journalist and an adjunct professor of communications at Insead.

Originally published in January 2007. Reprint R0701C

Index

You don't want to miss these...

We've combed through hundreds of *Harvard Business Review* articles on key management topics and selected *the* most important ones to help you maximize your own and your organization's performance.

10 Must-Read Articles on:

LEADERSHIP
How can you transform yourself from a good manager into an extraordinary leader?

STRATEGY
Is your company spending an enormous amount of time and energy on strategy development, with little to show for its efforts?

MANAGING YOURSELF
The path to your own professional success starts with a critical look in the mirror.

CHANGE
70 percent of all change initiatives fail. Learn how to turn the odds in your company's favor.

MANAGING PEOPLE
What really motivates people? How do you deal with problem employees? How can you build a team that is greater than the sum of its parts?

THE ESSENTIALS
If you read nothing else, read these 10 articles from some of *Harvard Business Review*'s most influential authors.

Harvard Business Review Press

Yours for only $24.95 each.
10 articles in each collection.
Available in PDF or paperback.

Order online at mustreads.hbr.org
or call us at 800-668-6780.
Outside the U.S. and Canada,
call +1 617-783-7450.